101 WAYS TO MAKE MONEY AT HOME

101 Ways to Make Money at Home

~ช่~

GWEN ELLIS

Servant Publications
Ann Arbor, Michigan

Vine Books is an imprint of Servant Publications especially designed to serve evangelical Christians.

This book is intended as an idea starter for establishing a work-from-home business. The ideas presented are not a guarantee of monetary success, since success can depend on initiative, ability, and determination to establish a from-home work situation. The information presented is based on research, examples, and advice from experts, trade associations, and business owners. Every effort has been made to present accurate information. The organizations, businesses, publications, products, services, and suppliers are given for information only and do not represent an endorsement by either the author or the publisher.

Published by Servant Publications
P.O. Box 8617
Ann Arbor, Michigan 48107

Cover design by Hile Illustration and Design, Ann Arbor, Michigan

96 97 98 99 00 10 9 8 7 6 5 4 3 2 1

Printed in the United States of America
ISBN 0-89283-898-1

Library of Congress Cataloging-in-Publiction Data

Ellis, Gwen
    101 ways to make money at home / Gwen Ellis.
      p.   cm.
    Includes bibliographical references and index.
    ISBN 0-89283-898-1
      1. Home-based businesses—United States. I. Title
HD2336.U5E45 1995
658'.041—dc20   95-52895
                                                      CIP

To my niece, Sherrill Ellis,
who, after a lengthy breakfast conversation,
took my ideas about establishing a gift basket business,
launched out, and established her own company.

Sherrill, I am so proud of you as you develop
a life for yourself
and your young son,
who also happens to be my great-nephew, Jordan.

CONTENTS

CHAPTER ONE

Is Working at Home Right for Me?

Posy Lough was a teacher who truly enjoyed her teaching. But when she became the mother of Kyser, she made a decision many women make today: to stay at home and be a full-time mother. She and Tom, her husband, have never regretted that decision.

Posy is an energetic, creative person. So, as time went on, she developed counted cross-stitch samplers of Bible verses and phrases. Her needlework began as a desire to strengthen her son's spiritual heritage, but as other families heard about her needlework products and activities for use at home, Posy's creative work quickly grew to a small mail-order business.

I first met Posy when she approached the company I worked for to see if we would market her designs. We were unable to do so, and for a couple of years I didn't hear from Posy.

When I talked with her recently, she told me she had changed directions somewhat and is now developing and marketing historical cross-stitch designs to museums and others who are interested in history.

Posy hires someone to design the cross-stitch patterns, while she finds new accounts and assembles the packets with the imprinted fabric, yarns, needles, and everything needed to complete the project. She and Tom keep track of their growing and extensive mailing list on computer. They also take photographs of the finished samplers and put together a catalog for their direct-mail list. With 100 different kits, it's more than a full-time job.

Posy and Tom run their business from home so they can be available to their son. They view the business as a way to fulfill their Christian family responsibilities and minister to other families. It works for the Lough family, and who knows what their young son is learning about running a business as he watches his parents cooperate on this venture?

GOING HOME

Posy is just one of thousands of people who are returning home to work. Women who fought hard to climb the corporate ladder have suddenly had enough and want to be home raising their children. Men who have grown weary of starched shirts, silk ties, and hours and hours of commute time are opting to dress in jeans or a jogging outfit and look out their windows at home while they work. The advent of personal computers, fax machines, and modems have made working from home a viable and attractive option for many.

An advertisement for a well-known cosmetic company states: "If you are career-oriented but are having unsettling thoughts about the toll your job is taking on your marriage and children, or your future family plans, starting your own business can give you the opportunity to put your priorities into better working order."[1]

If you're a mom or dad who aches to be there when the kids come home from school, or you're tired of boardrooms and corporate lunches, maybe there's another way to earn a living. Maybe you're a candidate for the newest trend of all— working from home.

THE UN-CORPORATE LADDER

Who would have thought fifteen years ago that men and women would want an alternative to climbing the corporate ladder? For years both sexes have fought, clawed, and struggled for recognition within their companies. Such magazines as *Working Woman, Entrepreneurial Woman, Success,* and *Inc.* thrived as people, especially women, sought information on management, what constituted sexual harassment, dressing for success, learning how to juggle a successful career and home life, and a lot of other work-related issues.

People still do a lot of corporate climbing, but some have had enough and are looking for alternative ways to contribute to family finances and support their children. *Barron's,* a business journal, calls the exodus of women from the workplace "a demographic sea-change." According to *Barron's,* "The two-paycheck family is on the decline; the traditional one-paycheck family is now the fastest-growing household unit."[2]

Why is this happening? First, women are tired of the harried, exhausted, chaotic lifestyle that often characterizes the two-career family. Second, many realize that little money is left after taxes, child-care, and expenses related to working. *Barron's* says that 80 percent of a woman's salary pays for these work-related costs: "By the time she pays for everything from pantyhose to transportation—sometimes in the form of a second car—working could become an expensive hobby."[3]

The Wall Street Journal was among the first to recognize an unusual trend in MBA training programs. They wrote,

The decline of interest by women in graduate business training reverses a trend and astonishes business schools, which are now scrambling to halt the slide. The share of women enrolled in many MBA programs has fallen 25 percent or more in recent years, admissions officials say. At

Northwestern University's Kellogg School, women constitute 27 percent of this fall's entering class, a 10-year low and a decline from a 37 percent peak in 1986. In the past year, Indiana University's graduate business school had a slide to 23 percent from 28 percent. This fall, Dartmouth's Tuck School enrolled 41 women—14 fewer than last year when the first year class was smaller.

[Elizabeth] Marinelli, a 26-year-old second-year student who heads the Columbia University School's Women in Business club... believes that many women link the MBA unfavorably to high-stress careers. "The issue of having a family is in the back of a lot of women's minds," she says. "They don't want to work 80 hours a week, so why go into something that requires it?"[4]

WORK-FROM-HOME ATTRACTIONS

There are many benefits to working from home. Here are just a few:

- You can take advantage of your most productive hours. We all have an internal clock, and the looser schedule of working from home lets us work with it rather than against it.

- You can't beat the commute. There are no car expenses or traffic hassles, and you can probably reduce your car insurance if you let your insurance agency know you are no longer commuting or that you are commuting less.

- You save time. Even if you put in a nine-hour day at home, you still have more time to spend with your family, since the average daily commute takes from forty-five minutes to two hours.

- You can pick your work environment. You can set up an office anywhere you like—outside, the basement, a spare bedroom, a loft, an office downtown.

- You save money. You save gas for commute, wear and tear on the car, child care, clothing, dry cleaning, lunches out.

- You get a tax break. You can take a percentage deduction on your mortgage or rent, phone, and all other utilities. (More about this later.)

- You have more flexibility in dividing personal and professional activities.

All of these benefits add up to increased job satisfaction and profitability.

I've been a manager of editorial projects for about fourteen years. I have to work within the rules and confines of the organization. But if I had my druthers, I'd give my editors a realistic deadline and tell them, "Go do it. I don't care where you do your assignment or when. You can edit this project standing on your head in the bathtub in the middle of the night. Just don't miss the deadline! And—it had better be well done."

Anne Studabaker, editor of *Profiles,* says: "Executive America, though increasingly receptive to augmenting the old ways of doing business, is still reluctant to let workers stay home. Fact is, most of those who do are more productive from a home office." She quotes Michael J. McDermott, who says, "Companies can save about $8,000 per telecommuter per year."[5]

While it is not always possible to let my employees work from home, I allow them as much freedom away from the confusion of the office as possible. I'm rewarded with excellent work, unbelievable loyalty, and contented employees.

WHAT ABOUT JOB SECURITY?

One reason for the increase in home business is that job security is almost nonexistent. Ask those who have spent the past twenty-five years climbing to the top of the corporate ladder, only to land in an out-placement service when the last rung gives way. Just yesterday I talked with a friend who thought she could keep her job for as long as she wanted it. Then the parent company wiped out the whole division in one fell swoop. She's out job hunting.

A recent article in *Time* magazine had a kicker that read, "Why should engineers be pumping gas?" The subhead: "Thirty months into a recovery, Americans are realizing that the great American job is gone. In its place: a new world of work."[6]

A common reason for layoffs is "reduction in force" or "right-sizing" (more commonly called "downsizing"). These terms simply mean that American companies are attempting to bring up the bottom line—make more money with fewer people. Managers have taken the brunt of this brutal slashing of the work force, and, says the *Time* article, American business is in trouble because it has slashed too far in cutting back management.

Even in a time of economic upturn, professionals, managers, highly skilled technicians, and office workers with seniority are standing in unemployment lines waiting to fill out paperwork. Prospects for the future don't look much brighter.

Forget any idea of career-long employment with a big company. Even after downsizing is carried to its logical—or illogical—extreme and the layoffs and early retirements stop, the corporate giants are not going to revert to hiring masses of long-term employees. They have discovered that it is more efficient and profitable to operate as contracting centers, buying goods and services from small companies rather than having them produced by their own employees, a process know as "outsourcing." The big corporation of the future will consist of a relatively small core of central employees and a mass of smaller firms working for it under contract. And even within the central core, there will be much shifting around, more hiring of people for specific, temporary assignments. "There are a whole lot more of us working for fees rather than for salaries," says Laurel Cutler, director of global marketing for the advertising giant Foote Cone Belding. "What you have seen is the end of work as marriage."[7]

When I moved to Seattle in 1973, there was a joke going around about a billboard at the edge of town that said, "Will the last person out of Seattle please turn out the lights?" You see, the city's economy rested upon one industry—Boeing aircraft manufacturing. Boeing had just executed a major downsizing.

I met a man who was a victim of that downsizing. After the layoff, he began an office-cleaning business. By the time I met him he'd been at it for a while, and the business was just beginning to take off. Now, twenty years later, he is still at it and feels that one of the best things that ever happened to him was being laid off from a corporate job. He's had freedom to develop his work environment and schedule it to suit him. He has job security—all offices have to be cleaned by somebody. He's had financial reward for a job well done; he has the satisfaction of being his own boss and running his own company successfully; and he's been able to give many college kids a hand up by providing them employment while they're in school.

If you've lost your job, think about a career change. One writer observes, "If you've lost your job today, you have the opportunity to do anything you want for the rest of your life."[8] It just may be that this is the time to think about doing something to make money from your home.

WHAT IF I'VE NEVER HAD A JOB?

Some of those needing to make extra money have never been in the workplace. Some are women who have raised a family and now find themselves with time on their hands and a desire to do something fun and creative with the rest of their lives.

Some women, who thought they were set for life, suddenly find themselves divorced or widowed, often with children to support and few skills for reentering the workplace. For these women it's not about making extra money, it's about making a livelihood.

For others, making money from home is about adding extra income for special things, such as private schooling for the kids, once-in-a-lifetime trips for the family, saving toward college or retirement, or purchasing a new home, furnishings, or car. They want to make a contribution to the family income while doing something they love. Whatever a person's reason for considering a work-from-home situation, he or she can find something meaningful to do.

One of my favorite books on the subject of working is *Do What You Love, the Money Will Follow* by Marsha Sinetar. The subtitle reads, "Discovering your right livelihood." I go through the book periodically to make sure I am still doing what I love most. I truly believe that if we are doing what we love, we will be productive, we will feel excited about our work, and our work will probably be profitable.

Doing what you love brings up the elemental question of finding your life's purpose. If you haven't yet figured that out, perhaps you should read no further until you do some serious thinking about why you are here on earth. Use the following foundational questions as a starting point.

1. What is my real life's purpose? (What do I want to have accomplished when I look back on my life in old age? Can I do that best in a corporate setting or working from home?)

2. How, specifically, would I have to think, speak, and act to bring that purpose into being? (What habits would I need to cultivate and what would I have to delete from my present life to live out my true purpose?)

3. What activities—what actual daily choices, attitudes, and concrete accomplishments—would I choose if I lived as if my purpose meant something to me? (If I were working from home, would I feel better about my choices and attitudes? Would the most important people in my life benefit from those better choices? Would I feel I was doing more to accomplish my life purpose?)

4. How would I live, daily, if I respected myself, others, and my life's purpose? (Do I feel my present job allows me to be myself? Do I respect myself, or do I feel I have to compromise myself where I now work?)[9]

THINKING THROUGH THE DECISION

If you know your life's purpose, and you simply want to find a way to accomplish it working from home, you're ready to evaluate how realistic working at home would be for you.

One of the first questions to answer is, "Do I know my work style?"[10] For instance, a friend told me she loves working in isolation. After two or three days she has to ask herself, "How long has it been since I've been out of the house?"

Another friend told me she goes almost crazy if she's alone too many hours, and she just has to get out of the house. In fact, she decided working from home was not for her because of this problem.

If you've been in the work world for a long time, how will you feel when you see your neighbors head off to their jobs? Free? Confused? Scared? Delighted? Relieved? Whatever else you feel, you'll probably also feel sidelined. For most new work-at-homers, there is a period of adjustment. For some, the adjustment is extended and severe; others make the adjustment rather quickly. So be prepared.

It helps if you're clear about the reasons you've decided to work from home. That's what we'll cover next in some excellent questions based on information by master planner and decision-maker, Bobb Biehl. You can use these questions any time you are contemplating a life-changing decision.

1. Can I write out, in one sentence, why I think working from home would be best for me and my family (if you have family living at home)?

2. Is this the best time to consider working from home? What would happen if I delayed the decision?

3. What key assumptions am I making? What do I assume it will cost to work from home? What do I assume will be the real benefits?

4. How will my decision to work from home affect my overall plan for my life? What difference will it make five, ten, twenty-five years from now?

5. Will my decision to work from home maximize my key strengths?

6. What facts should I have before I can make this decision with total confidence?

7. What trends, problems, or changes are necessitating this change? (Have you lost your job? Do you still have your job, but hate it? Is the job no longer what you want to do?)

8. What would my top three advisors say about this decision? Have I asked them?

9. Would I make the decision to work from home if I could get more money going to a regular job?

10. Have I been able to manage my finances in the past or, if I decide to work from home, will I need help in this area?

11. Am I disciplined enough to work at my from-home job every day?

12. Do I know where I can get support, both technical and emotional?[11]

When you have honestly asked and answered these questions, you're well on your way to discovering whether a from-home work enterprise is for you.

TIME TO THINK ABOUT WHAT YOU COULD DO

Let's assume you've decided you're a prime candidate for working from home. You have a great reason for wanting to do so, you know working alone is not a problem, and everything else seems to indicate it's time to earn money from home. Now what? Here are more assessment questions to fine-tune your decision to work from home.

1. What skills do you have? Are you great with kids? Do you like to make things with your hands? Are you a whiz-bang word processor? Do you understand accounting and taxes? What would bring you fulfillment and make work seem like play? If you've been in the workplace for a number of years and have honed your skill to perfection, is that skill transferable to the home workplace?

When a friend of mine got fired from her job, she felt the reasons for the firing were not valid and went to the unemployment agency to see what could be done. At that time in Washington state, where she lived, there was an innovative program in operation. Instead of doling out paychecks over an extended period of time, the unemployment office gave certain people a lump sum and training for establishing their own business. Candy took the offer and the classes. She bought a computer with her lump sum and went on doing just what she had been doing before getting fired, writing promotional copy for a number of large book publishing companies.

Candy transferred her skills to a home work situation. Working from home works great for her because she's a late starter in the morning and can work into the evening with ease. Most office jobs expect workers to be at their desks at 8:00 A.M. (If you think about the differences in our internal clocks, there probably is nothing less productive than asking a night person to produce excellent work in the morning.)

You may not be handed a lump sum to purchase equipment. Perhaps you will have to plan ahead for your departure from a job to a from-home work situation by slowly purchasing equipment and building a clientele. You can do this by accepting free-lance work as time allows before leaving your job.

2. **How could you transfer your skills to a work-from-home situation?** List ten ideas:

1. _____

2. _____

3. _____

4. _____

5. _____

6. _____

7. _____

8. _____

9. _____

10. _____

3. Can you fill a need with your product? Do you know how to do something well that no one else in your area is doing? One of the hot words in business these days is outsourcing. Outsourcing simply means that companies buy a service or a product outside of their own company to further their business. In the case of outsourcing products or parts, a company then assembles the product inside their plants into cars, airplanes, electronic devices, and lots of other things you would never think were the product of home businesses.

For example, my mom and dad have a cabin near a lake in Montana. Their neighbors are farmers and cattle ranchers, except for one man who proved that you can work from home, no matter where you live. His home was a small trailer near another lake that had spectacular beauty but was very isolated. His from-home business was quite specialized—repairing gauges for acetylene torches. When he'd made the repairs, he'd drive out to a location where he could send the gauge to his company, sixty miles away, and he'd pick up more gauges needing repair.

Think about some of the things you could make that would fill a need. List ten ideas in the space below:

1. _____

2. _____

3. _____

4. _____

5. _____

6. _____

7. _____

8. _____

9. _____

10. _____

4. **Do you see a need for a service?** I couldn't believe my eyes when I opened the local shopper's advertising paper and saw this ad:

POOP VAN SERVICE
#1 IN THE #2 BUSINESS
Cost: $14 per month
1 dog, 1 cleanup per week

Talk about finding a service need and filling it—or emptying it, in this case! Perhaps if I had a dog I'd consider using the service. Anyway, I admire this entrepreneur's creativity.

Think about a service need you could fill. List ten ideas below:

1. _____

2. _____

3. _____

4. _____

5. _____

6. _____

7. _____

8. _____

9. _____

10. _____

EXPECT TO MAKE MONEY

If you've done your homework and found a product or service the public truly wants, and if your skills are up to par, you can expect to make money. You have to make money or go back to work for someone else.

Whatever you've decided to do from home, it has to be business first. You can't allow distractions to alter your daily schedule; you must approach work from home in the same way you would a nine-to-five job. The advantage, of course, is that when you're working from home, you can take a break to put a load of clothes in the washer, start the dishwasher, move the sprinkler, let the dog out.

Launching a from-home business will take much more time than a forty-hour week, in most cases. Not only will you have to make the product or provide the service, you'll have to send out statements, do the banking, and collect your money. You will have to file papers, make phone calls, and write letters, unless you are telecommuting and have a secretary to do these things for you.

The reward for all of this is the potential for growth and earning. These are limited only by your own strength, staying capacity, and desire to grow.

I heard about a man who became an agent for photographers. Now, artistic types are good at their craft, but the very thing that makes them good artists often makes it difficult for them to make money. This man saw a need and stepped in with his computer to be a liaison between the photographers and those who use photography. He would contact a magazine to see what type of photography they wanted for a particular issue. Then he'd go to his data bank and see which photographer or pictures he could suggest to supply the need.

This man was not a great artist, but he was good with detailed information and knew how to maximize his computer skills. Reportedly, he made in excess of $400,000 in one year.

Everybody wins in a situation like this. The publications do not have to search for the photographers, the photographer doesn't have to search for a place to peddle his photos, and the agent provides a service for which he is well paid.

If you think you see a need no one else is filling, first talk it up with those who could use your services. A colleague came to me the other day and asked, "What would you think about a from-home business in which I made the contacts between editors, writers, photographers, typesetters, and printers for publishing houses?" As the managing editor of a severely understaffed operation dependent upon freelance help, I was excited at the very idea. I was ready to start giving her business.

After my enthusiastic response, my colleague talked with another friend who had started her own company several years ago. She offered the same kind of enthusiasm and said that if such a brokerage existed, she would be using it on a regular basis. But she added some advice. "Start now. Start building your clientele while you are still working. Gather the equipment you'll need and begin in your off-hours to build your business."

By talking to a number of people and networking, my colleague has begun to gather information, gain ideas, and structure her dream. I hope she goes ahead with her plan.

The Amway Corporation is a master in encouraging the work-from-home idea. Most of those who have become quite successful in Amway started on-the-side businesses and kept their regular jobs while they built their clientele. When their at-home businesses became larger and more productive than their jobs, they launched full from-home operations, and devoted all their energies to them.

This book contains ideas for making extra money from home and stories of people who have done it successfully. I am convinced that the next great idea is just around the corner, waiting to be discovered by somebody who doesn't want to punch a time clock and who wants to find another way to make money. It's exciting to think that one of those ideas might just come from someone reading this book.

In the next chapter we will look at how to set up a plan for working from home. We'll talk about equipment you'll need, creating a work space, how much you hope to make the first year, and more.

Are you ready?

CHAPTER TWO

Making a Plan

Before you begin any kind of work from home, you need to plan your venture from beginning to end. The plan becomes a road map for future development, a checklist for things to accomplish, and a measuring stick to see how your business is doing. The plan can be as informal or formal as you want to make it.

Traditional business plans have four parts. They are:

1. A definition of your business

2. A marketing plan

3. A production plan

4. A financial plan

These four elements will guide you toward success. They will force you to ask hard questions *before* you begin your from-home work and will keep you from getting in over your head without a plan of rescue after you begin your business.

Before you sit down to brainstorm and construct your business plan, consider the following questions. Your answers may affect your planning.

Where will you live?

If you are working from home, you can pretty much pick the city and locale where you wish to live. You can choose to live near parents or in a town with a church that has an excellent youth program or in an area that has ministry needs your family can meet. But first consider if there are enough customers where you wish to live. If your business is a product,

consider if you would have access to the raw materials to manufacture your product. Other issues are the cost of living in the
city of your choice and if you would make enough income to
live there.

Telluride, Colorado, is one of the vacation destinations of
America. If I want to go to Telluride from where I live, I must
drive most of the day. Yet Telluride is full of people who work
for large corporations, write books, and head all kinds of businesses. The workers are telecommuting—using fax machines,
modems, telephones, pagers, videos, teleconferencing, and
other communication devices and methods to live where they
wish and still do the business they love. Occasionally these
people fly out to meet with customers or vendors or to attend
corporate meetings. Today you can probably set up your business and live almost anywhere you like.

*How many hours a day are you willing to put into your work-
from-home venture?*

It takes determination and drive to make a from-home business succeed. Because from-home ventures tend to attract dri-
ven, highly creative people who are willing to take risks and
launch out on their own, it also attracts people who may be
addicted to work. You have to set limits on your time so that
the needs of your from-home venture do not consume you.

If you are a mother of young children and decide to work
from home so that you can be with them, you'll have to set
limits on the amount of time you spend working or you'll end
up having less time with them.

Combining business and family is a great idea, but to make
it work, "You have to be disciplined; you need to have the
unswerving support of your family, and you must present a
professional image."

Georganne Fiumara, founder of Mothers' Home Business
Network, cautions: "For women who operate their business

from home, being able to be at hand for their children is a major motive for becoming an entrepreneur in the first place. But it will be difficult."[1]

If you intend to take care of your business and your children at the same time, you may end up spending time in your office between midnight and 5:00 A.M.

What kind of plan do you need?

Depending on the size of the work-from-home operation you hope to set up, the plan can be as simple or complex as you want to make it. If you want to make gift baskets in your basement, you can probably put together a plan on the back of an envelope. (Although you'd probably want to convert it to something more permanent after a while.) You don't need to follow the order I've outlined in this chapter. Start the plan with something easy to grasp, such as "How much money do I want to make?" Now let's take a close look at the parts of a business plan.

DEFINITION OF THE BUSINESS

Overview. Many people who are considering working from home really don't know what kind of business they want. They may tell you they're in mail order or housecleaning or accounting, but they don't have a specific, action-oriented definition of their enterprise. It's pretty easy to define your business if you're making and selling something, such as gift baskets. It gets a little more complicated if you're in a service business where there is no product to sell. In every case you are exchanging something for money. You are selling something—either a product, your knowledge and expertise, or your labor.

To help define your business, see if you can do these tasks.

1. Write a description of the business you want to begin.

2. List the products or services you will be selling.

3. Describe who will use your products or services.

4. List your major competitors.

You must be able to describe in a couple of sentences your vision for your business. This is often called a mission statement. While it may seem like busywork to go through the exercise of writing a mission statement, it will guide your business for the rest of its existence. Mission statements, however, are not cast in iron and can be changed as the business develops. In fact, they should be reviewed yearly and updated if necessary. (To define your business in detail, use the Business Plan Worksheet[2] at the end of this chapter. You probably will not complete it in one sitting, but will return to it again and again as you progress through this book.)

What are the legal ramifications of starting a home-based business?

I had dinner with friends not long ago. One of the two was at a crossroads in her life and considering a from-home work situation. This was one of the most capable women I know, and yet I heard her asking, "What do I do? What legal papers do I have to file? Do I need a city license?"

Many potential work-from-home people are scared off by the legalities of permits, licenses, incorporations, and other legal procedures. If you're one of them, don't despair, but do follow through.

The Small Business Administration (SBA) has a ton of information to walk you through the legal entanglements. Call them at 1-800-368-5855 or write them at SBA-Publications, P.O. Box 30, Denver, Colorado 80201-0030, and get a listing of their inexpensive pamphlets that deal with every aspect of setting up your own business. (There is a partial listing of pamphlet topics in chapter 11.)

Another source of information for starting and running your own business is your local chamber of commerce. The chamber can give you specific information on legalities for your area.

For the purposes of this book, the important thing to remember is that you can't avoid the legal issues. You must face them and you need to know it's not as intimidating as you may think. Look around at the immigrants who are operating businesses and doing well. If they can navigate the murky waters of our legal system—with the handicap of language barriers, cultural differences, and a host of other negatives—so can you!

Let's briefly look at some of those legalities.

Zoning. Most cities and towns have zoning laws that dictate what kinds of businesses can be conducted out of a home, and whether businesses can be conducted at all. This is to protect homeowners and maintain property values. No one wants to live next to a wrecking yard.

Most nonpolluting, low-traffic kinds of businesses are allowed, but before you set up shop, do a thorough investigation to find out what is approved for your area.

At one time my brother ran a construction business out of his home. He used only subcontractors to do his work. Their trucks and equipment were never at his home for more than a few minutes in the mornings while they received instructions for the day. However, the neighbors began to complain about the number of vehicles sitting around his house. What the neighbors failed to take into consideration was that my brother had three teenage daughters, who had their own cars, living at home. The cars in front of the house had nothing to do with his business. He had done the proper legal work. If those vehicles had been part of his business, even though he was legal, things might have become very sticky for him.

If your business conforms to existing zoning laws, you are free to begin your from-home work, but stay abreast of anything that might change zoning laws. If there is a neighborhood association, join it as a way to keep your ear to the ground and assess your neighbors' attitudes about your business.

If you don't meet zoning requirements, things become a little more difficult. Neighbors and zoning boards are most concerned that your business will be messy, create traffic, noise, or parking problems. If you can convince them otherwise, you will probably be able to obtain the permit you need.

You might be able to change your business enough to conform it to the laws. If your zoning rule says you can't have employees coming to work at your home, see if they can do work from their own homes.

If you want to take on city hall, you might be able to change zoning laws that have not kept up with the return of the worker to his own home, either as a telecommuter or in establishing his own business from home.

Sole Proprietorship, Partnership or Corporation? Another legal decision you must make is the form your business will take. You have three options: sole proprietorship, partnership, or corporation.

A *sole proprietorship* is the least costly and least complicated way to set up your business. Remember that a sole proprietorship is totally dependent upon your ability to work and have good ideas for growth. There is no other person in the business to rely on.

A *partnership* happens when two or more entrepreneurs form a company. Legal fees for setting up such an arrangement are usually more costly than those required for a sole proprietorship and less costly than a corporation.

The up side of a partnership is more capital for growth and

more ideas for how to grow the business. The downside is getting rid of a bad partner.

A *corporation* is the most complicated and most costly of the three options. The ongoing accounting, legal, and tax-reporting obligations of a corporation are much more complicated than for the other two options. Corporations have boards, shareholders, and shared responsibility for the business. It is necessary to keep everyone informed of decisions, the company's financial status, and a host of other actions.

One category of incorporation is known as the "Sub-S Corporation" or simply "S Corporation." A Sub-S Corporation can be established if all the shareholders (owners) consent, if it is a domestic corporation, and has no more than thirty-five shareholders, all of whom are both citizens and residents of the United States.

One of the greatest advantages of this type of incorporation is that the shareholders can avoid double taxation (at both corporate and shareholder levels) on the profits of the business. In the early years of the business, owners of these types of incorporations who are active in managing the business can often deduct any loss of income (when expenses exceed income) from their personal income tax.

To learn more about Sub-S corporations, or about any of these types of classifications, it is wise to seek the advice of a tax attorney in the beginning of your work-from-home situation in order to avoid serious problems later on. An attorney will guide your decision about what legal form your company should take.

Other Regulations. You will need to file the name of your business with the County Clerk and to acquire the necessary tax and sales tax identification numbers and authorizations from state tax and revenue authorities. You'll need an Employer Identification Number (EIN) even if you are the only employee of your company. Some cities have local requirements as well. Once again, your attorney should be able to help you.

If the legalities seem overwhelming and threaten to sink your ship of dreams, hang in there. One day you'll have met the requirements and your business will be thriving.

MARKETING PLAN

Overview: How are you going to market your product or service? Many great ideas have died along the way because the creators of those ideas didn't answer this question or only had a foggy notion where they would sell their goods or services.

Two years ago I made Christmas stockings for my daughter, her roommates, and my son. Their enthusiasm and the enthusiasm of friends who saw them made me think I could get rich making and selling one-of-a-kind Christmas stockings.

I knew that in order to make a profit, I had to keep expenses down. So I bought a number of velvet, taffeta, and satin dresses at a thrift shop and tore them to pieces. The dresses might have been worn once to a wedding or other special event. The fabric was almost new. I also bought ribbons, lace, and other decorative trims at the thrift shop. The money I invested was minimal.

The expensive part was my time, but I thought it would be creative and fun, so I set up my sewing machine and sewed after work in the evenings. It wasn't long until I had a big pile of stockings. That was the fun part. Now, how was I going to sell them?

We have a yearly Christmas boutique where I work, and I thought that would be a good place to display my wares. People came, people looked, people exclaimed, people did not buy. That boutique had been my sole marketing plan.

I quickly regrouped and took the stockings to a craft consignment shop in our little town and eventually sold about twelve stockings. I didn't make much money, but I did learn a lot about having a plan and a backup plan. I didn't lose anything but some time, but if my sole objective had been to make money, I would have been sorely disappointed.

I learned something else by showing my wares at that craft show. I saw what was selling, and in this case it was cinnamon rolls and hot salsa. The seller of the salsa had tortilla chips and samples of the sauce available for tasting. She also had a business card—a link to filling orders after the show ended. She wisely used this one-time event to help grow her from-home business.

To succeed in a from-home business, you must ask all the necessary questions, analyze the market, and try to make a realistic projection of sales. After careful analysis, some things that look good in the beginning may not seem so profitable and may not be worth your time.

Consider this partial list of questions to help you decide if there is a market where you live for the goods or services you wish to provide:

1. What is the consumer's attitude toward businesses like the one I am planning?

2. What do I know about how my intended customers shop and buy?

3. Is the price of my product or service in line with what my intended customers want to pay?

4. How broad is my market?

5. If I am appealing to only a part of the market, is that segment big enough to sustain my business?

6. Who are my competitors?

7. What are my competitors' strengths and weaknesses?

8. Have any of those companies gone out of business? Why?

9. Are my competitors' businesses growing or shrinking?

10. What do I have to offer that they do not? Can I compete?

To further help you brainstorm, consider the following:

Do I already have customers?

Make a list of individuals and companies who have seen your product or who have talked with you about your services. Be realistic. When it comes to putting money on the table, who can you truly count on? How consistently will they need your product or service? Would it be possible to draw up a contract with customers to assure their business? Are there highs and lows in the business you've chosen?

Recently a friend lost her job through an unusual series of events not at all due to any lack of ability. In fact, she's almost a specialist in editing children's books. Since I needed some free-lance help, I called to encourage her and to offer work. She told me she was seriously considering continuing as a free-lancer and was not seeking another job. Because I am familiar with her work and expertise, I was able to suggest several others who might use her services.

Since she had one paying customer—our company—who was willing to give her more work and to recommend her to others, she could consider herself launched as a free-lance editor.

What customers do you already have? Do you have at least one or two you can count on for steady business?

Where will I make my sale?

Will you set up a stand beside the road? Will you go to an office building to peddle your wares? Will you clean houses in a small town or go to a neighboring larger city? Where are your customers?

One elderly lady doesn't wait for business to come to her; she goes to offices around town with a basket of bagels and a box of Danish rolls, croissants, and other kinds of pastries. She only comes to our office once a week, and she sells nearly everything she brings. Workers plan for their Thursday morning treat. I don't know how much money she makes, but it must be enough pocket money to make the effort worth her time. The point is, whether you are selling Danishes or parts for rocket engines, you will have to get out and sell your product to the customers, and you will have to know where they are.

How do I plan to let people know about my service or product?

The answer to this question may be the most important one in your plan. Years ago a product developer at the 3M Company developed by accident the adhesive for Post-it notes. He realized that although it was a mistake, he was on to something important. The advertising plan was simple. The company sent a couple of pads to the executive secretaries of all the Fortune 500 companies, and the rest, as they say, is history.

The secretaries began to show and tell other secretaries, which created demand, and the sales poured in. Can you imagine life without Post-it notes and all their look-alikes?

Strive to achieve word-of-mouth advertising. Not only is it free, it's also the most effective kind of advertising. Could you give something away—like hot salsa on a chip—in order to get everyone talking about your product? Could you do such a fantastic job with your service that people started talking about it? Could you provide extra touches that build your reputation for excellence? For example, if your from-home business is cleaning houses, what would happen if you left a tiny bouquet of fresh flowers in the houses you clean? Wouldn't that set you apart from other housecleaners and start people talking about your business?

You will have to find ways to let people know about your service or product, but the basic way is to buy advertising. To be effective, run ads consistently. Remember the Poop Van Service ad in chapter 1? It runs, week after week, in a *Little Nickel* advertising paper. This is one of the cheapest kinds of advertising. The ad has a cute picture of a spotted dog and is highly recognizable. Do you think people see this ad? Yes. Do you think they recognize it and know what it advertises at a glance? Yes.

It pays to advertise. If something has to be cut from a budget, make advertising the last thing to go. Advertising accomplishes two important things for the work-from-home person:

1. *It informs.* It lets others know what the work-from-home person is offering.

2. *It provides a service.* Ads are matchmakers, bringing together people looking for a product or service and the seller of that product or service.

PRODUCTION PLAN

Overview. When you know what you are selling because you have defined your business, and when you know the market to which you are selling—its size, location, and buying habits—then you are ready to think about how to manufacture the product you are selling. Here are some questions to get you going.

1. What inventory and operating supplies will I need?

2. Do I know how much I will have to manufacture? The quality? The technical specifications? The price range?

3. Do I know the sources of raw materials I will need?

4. Do I know the price ranges for each product from my suppliers?

5. Do I know the credit terms of each supplier?

6. Will the supplier's price allow me to make an adequate markup on my product and still remain competitive?

Also consider:

What kind of equipment will I need?

If you are baking, you need bowls, spoons, an oven, and so on. If you are caring for children you need safety fences, blankets, toys, and food for meals. If you are repairing cars, you need wrenches, screwdrivers, and replacement parts. If you are writing, editing, doing accounting, or doing mail order, you need a computer.

What equipment do I already have?

If you are converting a hobby into a business, you may already have some of the equipment you need to work from home. Perhaps you've been an amateur photographer and enjoyed developing your own film. Over the years, you've bought equipment. Now you want to start a from-home photography business. You probably already have a good portion of the equipment you need to get started.

Maybe you want to start a from-home business of dressmaking. You have a sewing machine, iron, and scissors. Perhaps all you need to add is a dressmaker's form.

THE FINANCIAL PLAN

Overview. Now that you know the cost to produce your goods or services, who and where your market is, and exactly what your business is about, you are ready to make some income and expense projections. The primary purpose of a financial plan is to know how much money you will need to begin and sustain your business. To make sales projections that are realistic, don't overestimate your profit and don't underestimate your expenses.

Your monthly projected income will be offset by expenses, often hidden ones. An accountant can help you identify what those are and show you how to prepare for them.

Don't forget start-up costs, which include everything from a deposit on the telephone, decorating your office, and

Mistakes to Avoid

Too often we hinder our own efforts by making no plan. Here are some reasons businesses do not make it.

1. *Failure to plan your from-home work.* Some people spend more time planning a vacation than they do planning their from-home business. You need a business plan—a "road map"—as you integrate all the little bits and pieces of your ideas, aspirations, and dreams. A plan helps you put the puzzle pieces together. Without a plan, you have no direction and you probably won't achieve what you set out to do.

2. *Failure to implement the plan you've developed.* Many, even after they make a plan, fail to put it into action. Just as a family budget is a plan for spending money, a work-from-home plan is a guide for making money and planning expenses. If you were to plot a trip on a map and then put the map in the car trunk and never refer to it, you might find yourself wandering in circles.

purchasing equipment, to printing stationery and business cards. Plan for your living expenses. That means putting aside enough capital to sustain you and your family while you are getting your business income up and running. This will be a cash-poor, difficult time, but it will be easier if you plan for it by having enough capital for a year's living expenses.

Also consider:

How much money do I want to make?

What are your financial needs? Are you trying to earn a

---

3. *Failure to organize financial records.* Keeping track of every transaction you make is essential. You have to be able to substantiate your earnings or losses to the IRS. Careful records will make this task easier.

4. *Failure to seek professional help.* Unless you're an accounting whiz, one of the first people you should see when starting a work-from-home operation is an accountant. He or she will guide you in setting aside enough money for taxes, make sure you are paying the correct amount of social security tax, and guide you in what fees to pay if you have anyone working for you.

In an article in *Family Circle*, author Mary Rowland writes about why some women who have set out to work from home fail. She says, "Many women are inclined to think they must go it alone. They are leery of asking for professional help; they're afraid to give up a piece of the business to a partner or another investor, even if that might be the best way for the enterprise to grow. Those who have succeeded emphasize that you must overcome these fears and rely on professionals who will explain things to you in a very basic way."[3]

living from home? To supplement a spouse's income? To earn a little money for extras? Are you trying to achieve a certain financial goal? Is it a long-term or short-term financial goal?

How long will it take to make money?

Whatever your financial needs and goals, it will take time to get your from-home-money-making idea going. How long can you wait to make a profit? How long do you think it will take before you have enough customers to begin making a profit? How long will it take to pay back your initial investment of equipment and set-up? Take that estimate of time and double it.

For most people, it takes twice as long as they thought it would to turn a profit. For that reason many give up before they find success. It takes determination to stay with it.

How much money will I need for equipment?

If, after you've taken inventory, you realize you'll have to purchase some equipment, decide what equipment is absolutely essential. Long ago my father told me that the right tool makes the job easier. For a long time I tried to get by with inadequate tools, but I finally began to acquire the tools I needed for my projects, and I discovered my father was right.

Will I need ongoing accounting help?

An accountant can save time, watch for pitfalls, and make sure you are paying the necessary fees and taxes. He or she can set up a quarterly tax and social security payment structure to avoid a huge payment at the end of the year.

Besides a CPA, you will need a bookkeeper to keep accurate records. Perhaps you will be the bookkeeper in the beginning. There are some great software programs to help you. Two of those programs are Quicken, a checkbook system, and Quickbooks, a program devised to streamline bookkeeping.

What about insurance? How much will it cost?

Unfortunately, there's one more not-something-we-like-to-talk-about item in a work-from-home plan—insurance. Many people have lost their money-making enterprises because a product they've sold was defective. They were sued, and because they did not have adequate insurance, they found themselves out of business.

If you have an inventory of product you have created; if you have customers coming to your home; if you use expensive equipment for your at-home venture; if you distribute someone else's products; if you care for other people—children or the elderly—you need to adequately protect yourself from lawsuits.

If you are not under the health, personal, and life insurance of a company plan (and you won't be unless you are telecommuting), you have to take care of insurance needs. Just what would happen to you, your family, and your from-home venture if you were sick or injured? If it is true that most accidents happen at home, then you need to consider carefully what kinds of insurance you need now that your home and workplace are the same.

There are four essential kinds of insurance: fire, liability, automobile, and worker's compensation. Let's look briefly at each one.

Fire. You most certainly have fire insurance on your home, but when you bring your work home, check with your insurance agent to see what additional coverage you will need for office and equipment associated with your business, inventory, and hazards caused by the home business, such as explosion, vandalism, and malicious mischief. Be accurate with your agent when you confer with him. It hurts to pay the increased insurance premiums, but it hurts more to attempt to recover from a loss associated with fire.

Liability. Liability limits of $1 million are not out of line in our litigation-happy society. Such policies cover bodily injury, libel, and slander. If you do most of your from-home work away from home, as is the case in sales, your liability insurance should cover you there as well.

Automobile. You probably have automobile insurance, but if you now own vehicles used for business, or if an employee or subcontractor uses a car or truck for your business, you can be liable even though you don't own the vehicle. Your automobile insurance agent is your best friend in keeping you from either going broke or being sued because of an accident.

Worker's compensation. If you are the only employee of your work-from-home business, you will not need worker's compensation. The moment you hire another employee, you will. The law requires that you provide employees with a safe place to work, that you hire competent people, provide safe tools, and warn employees of existing dangers. Accidents can and do happen. Do not neglect worker's compensation insurance.

In addition to these essential insurance coverages, there are some other kinds you may want to consider, such as business interruption insurance, crime insurance, product and service liability insurance, and floater coverage, which is an extension of your basic fire insurance. This covers everything from computers to expensive art work and has a separate premium for each piece.

If you have employees, then you must think about their insurance needs as well. You may need to offer group health insurance, disability insurance, key-man life insurance, which is payable to the company in the event a key employee dies, and retirement income.

If you are confused about your insurance needs, consult a professional broker or contact the Home-Based Business

Institute, 138 Hillair Circle, White Plains, New York, 10605
(914) 946-6600.

IT'S A GOOD PLAN TO HAVE A GOOD PLAN

You'll never be sorry you took the time to think through a
plan carefully for your from-home business. This plan will
become a beacon in dark times and a milestone in the good
times.

If you think you're ready to plunge into from-home work
without giving it much thought, slow down, count the cost,
estimate the profit, and then go forward.

Now let's look at some from-home business ideas.

Business Plan Worksheet[4]

As you continue reading this book, the answers to each of these questions will emerge, so consider your Business Plan a document-in-progress at this point. For now, leave blank any questions you aren't sure about. You should turn here again and again as you move closer to starting a home-based business.

1. Describe the business in detail:

Company Name: _____

Address: _____

_____

Owner: _____

Legal Structure: _____
(Attach copies of legal documents to your business plan.)

2. State the major goals and objective of the business:

_____

_____

_____

3. Discuss the special skills and experiences you bring to the company. Describe your qualifications. (Attach a resume to your business plan.)

_____

_____

_____

4. Describe the products or services offered.

_____

_____

_____

5. What advantages do your products or services have over those already on the market?

_____

_____

_____

6. Describe your market (those people most likely to buy your product or service).

_____

_____

_____

7. List current customers, if any.

_____

_____

_____

8. Indicate when, where and how you plan to advertise and publicize your business.

_____

_____

_____

9. List all equipment and supplies you will require to get started.

_____

_____

_____

10. Indicate how much money you will need to start. Beside these figures, project how you will obtain it. (Attach a copy of your start-up and first-year budgets.)

Amount   **Funding Source**

_____   _____

_____   _____

_____   _____

_____   _____

_____   _____

_____   _____

_____   _____

CHAPTER THREE

Simple Work-from-Home Ideas

C hester Greenwood, of Farmington, Maine, was fifteen years old and tired of his ears feeling half-frozen. So he asked his mother to sew fur onto two ear-shaped loops of wire in order to keep his ears from turning blue. When he hooked his fur-covered wire loops on a bowler hat, "Chester's ear protectors" were invented. As soon as his friends got a look at his ear protectors, his mother busily sewed more for all the neighborhood kids to wear when they skated.

In 1877, Chester was granted a patent for his invention. By now he had improved the design by adding a spring to fit over the head. As so often happens, his from-home business, resulting from an innovative idea, took off. More and more customers demanded more and more earmuffs and Chester and many others earned a living for the rest of their lives.

When he died at age seventy-nine, Chester's earmuff factory still operated full time. His great idea continues to this day, as earmuffs have regained their popularity in recent years.

LET'S BRAINSTORM

I've been amazed while researching ideas for this book at the kinds of from-home work people do and the creativity they show. I'm convinced that ideas for successful from-home work are limited only by a person's imagination. Some of you reading this book are sitting on ideas that could be as beneficial to mankind as Chester's earmuffs, and you just need a push to get going. Some of you need the practical advice in this book to get you launched. And some of you just need to brainstorm possible ideas. That's what we're going to do in this chapter.

Using the information you've learned in the first two chapters about your skills, available finances, needed work space, time, strength, and desire to work from home, spend a few minutes writing down every possible work idea you can do from home. No ideas? Then read on.

LITTLE OR NO MONEY TO INVEST

If you have little or no money and no equipment, look to the service industry as a place to start working from home. Perform a helpful service, do it well, do it at a reasonable price, and the customers will come.

I heard about a woman in my city who provides a bill-paying service. What comes around more often than writing those checks? Busy executives, working women, and housewives who'd rather do something else with their time pay this woman to pay their bills.

What kind of equipment would you need to provide a bill-paying service? A checkbook and a pen. What kind of expertise do you need? Some basic math skills. Probably you would also need to get bonded, and you would have to build a high level of trust and confidentiality to be trusted with information about your customers' finances. It's not such a far-fetched idea, however.

Remember, if you're looking for a from-home work opportunity, first look at your marketable skills and then assess what equipment you already have to do the job. For instance, do you have a watering can or a vacuum cleaner? You can go into business. Do you have an oven or a telephone? You can begin working from home. Let me list some service businesses that require little money up front.

Plant Care
Start-up cost: $500-$5,000 (liability insurance, classified ads or flyers)
Break-even: About one year
Annual income: $10,000 to $55,000

If you have a small ladder, a watering can—or an old coffee can and a bucket—and some knowledge of plants, you can begin a plant-care business. Every office building, hospital, restaurant, and clinic in the country has plants. They clean the air, provide a decorative touch, and give confined office workers, patients, and patrons a touch of the outdoors. Somebody has to take care of all those plants.

A couple in Washington state started a from-home plant care business. Their clients included restaurants, hospitals, apartment buildings, offices, and even private homes. They estimated they could accommodate up to seventy clients without hiring additional staff. Rather than expanding the business, they have chosen to keep their clientele to a number they can handle alone. They grossed $20,000 their first year. Now, twelve years later, they gross $100,000 a year. Not bad!

Many of their clients have very expensive plants, so they insist on sole control of watering, feeding, and all other maintenance. Their policy is to replace any plant that dies while in their care. A person just starting out in the plant-care business might not be able to give such a guarantee, but it's a goal worth setting.

If you have obtained the necessary business license and filled out the paperwork for your plant-care business, you will have a tax number that enables you to buy plants at wholesale prices.

If you think plant-care might be for you, answer the following questions:

1. What businesses in my area could I approach about caring for their plants?
2. What do I know about caring for plants?
3. What don't I know?
4. Where will I learn it?
5. How much will I charge? (Set a minimum fee and hold to it. A suggested fee is $1.25 to $1.50 per plant per visit. It still takes time and gasoline to get to the site, whether you're caring for five plants or twenty-five. The couple from Washington charges from $55 to $800 a month.)[1]

You can inform potential customers about your plant service by

- running a small ad in the service section of your newspaper or in business publications in your area,
- volunteering to speak at local Kiwanis or Rotary clubs about plants,
- mailing a flyer to all the hospitals and businesses in your town,
- getting on the radio to do a call-in talk show about plants,
- telling everyone you know about your business and handing them a distinctive business card.

Specialty Dressmaker

Start-up cost: $500 (assuming you have a sewing machine and other sewing supplies) for business cards, liability insurance, advertising
Break-even: Six months to one year
Annual income: $30,000 to $50,000

You can charge $20-$30 per hour or charge by the project for custom sewing. Check out several specialty sewing shops in your area and ask what they charge. Here are some custom sewing categories and questions about those categories to consider.

Wedding Dresses
1. Do I know how much wedding dresses cost?
2. Do I know how long it takes to order and receive a wedding dress?
3. Can I effectively handle the concerns of a bride who has either gained or lost weight before the wedding (and the possibility of time-consuming alterations)?
4. Do I know how to plan carefully enough to ensure the dress will arrive on time for the wedding?

You can use all these concerns to your advantage as a dressmaker and make wedding dresses successfully from your home. You only need an iron and ironing board, a sewing machine, and a sewing room or area in your home where fabrics would be safe from soiling while you construct the dress. If you sew well enough to even consider the idea, you probably already have all these items in your home.

Think what a wonderful service you could provide. Your customers wouldn't have to order months in advance from some far-off company; they wouldn't have to worry about last-minute fittings and who was going to do them, because you'd be right there in the same town. You could even go to the church on the wedding day to make any last-minute adjustments.

Advertise by telling local pastors and wedding coordinators about your services, by running an ad in the services section of your newspaper, and by putting up flyers in places where young women congregate—college bulletin boards, church youth groups. See if you can get on local television as a bridal gown expert. Have some brides model the gowns you made for them.

Costumes
Costumes and skating outfits are specialty items. A skating costume must fit the skater perfectly. It must not bind or constrict in any way. Nothing must come loose and fall on the ice

during a performance, and each costume must be completely different from every other costume on the ice. Imagine the excitement a specialty dressmaker might feel in seeing one of her costumes on a world-class skater as he or she competes for a gold medal.

Sharon, a friend of mine, loves to make skating costumes. She started sewing them when her daughter, a figure skater, needed costumes. All those gorgeous, glittery ice-skating costumes are handmade and very expensive. Sharon decided to make the costumes herself and discovered she loves to do beadwork. She can sit for hours in the evenings, after finishing her regular job, and endlessly sew those tiny beads and sequins onto costumes.

Though the market for world-class ice skating costumes might be limited, there's quite a market for historical reproduction costumes for local and regional pageants, regional ice pageants, and musical and dance reviews. If your county or town is planning a historical celebration, join the committee to see what costumes they will need and make a bid to provide them.

Musicians, dancers, and singers also need specialty costumes, many of which require beading and sequins. To find the market, check with other dressmakers and tailors in your town, contact the wardrobe departments of festivals, plays, pageants, galas, and celebrations. Advertise in the telephone directory under "costumers," in the local papers, and in those papers catering to the show-biz trade. You could also make a fabulous spangled costume and exhibit it in a parade with a sign showcasing the name of your business.

Other Specialty Sewing
Alterations
Custom clothing for both men and women
Custom pants
Color coordinating, wardrobe consulting, fabric shopping

Wallpapering and Painting

Start-up cost: $750 for advertising, business cards and flyers, basic wallpapering equipment, ladders, liability insurance
Break-even: Immediate to two months
Annual income: $12,000-$100,000

Wallpapering

A colleague of mine does wallpapering in his spare time to supplement his regular income. He's done it long enough that he can paper a room in an evening or on a Saturday afternoon.

Wallpapering requires simple equipment:

- a plastic bin for wetting the paper
- a razor blade or other cutting tool
- a straight edge of some kind
- a chalk line
- a ruler
- a roller for rolling down the seams
- a large brush for easing out air bubbles

If you are applying wallcovering that requires paste, you'll need a brush to apply the glue. The cost for equipment is about $25 and it can be used again and again.

If you don't know much about wallpapering but like the idea, some wallpaper stores give classes, others offer video training, and some even have demonstrations and hands-on practice areas. Practice at home for a while, and when you think you've got it right, go back to the store and ask them if you can post a notice about your services or be on their referral list of installers.

When you start your wallpapering business, call several businesses in your area and ask what they charge. Start your fees somewhere in the middle of the price range. As your business grows, you can raise your prices.

Keep your name in the customers' minds by periodically

sending flyers or business cards. Word of mouth is still the best advertising, and if you do a great job, do it quickly, show up when you said you would, and price the job fairly, you will find customers.

Painting

Basic equipment:

- an assortment of paint brushes, rollers, pad painters
- masking tape
- drop cloths
- rags
- ladders
- paint scrapers
- sanding equipment
- razor blades for scraping paint off windows

For exterior painting invest in a power sprayer. It's more costly but should last a long time.

Dog Maintenance

Start-up cost: $1,000 for business cards, small ad in newspapers, grooming table, cages, sinks
Break-even: Six months to a year
Annual income: $15,000 to $25,000

If you like dogs and have a big tub, a sink, or even a bathtub, you can clean up on dogs. It's a dirty job, but somebody's going to get paid to do it, and it could be you.

Dog maintenance ranges from giving fancy haircuts to giving a monthly or bi-weekly bath to just combing the dog's hair. For the purposes of this book, let's limit dog maintenance to washing, brushing, and grooming. Lots of people have dogs with long hair and it has to be brushed, combed, and cut periodically.

Many people would happily pay someone to do it. You'll need:

- a tub
- towels
- a hair dryer
- dog grooming clippers
- a grooming table
- various brushes and combs
- a couple of holding cages to contain the animals until their owners come for them.

A new trend in pet grooming is the mobile grooming service. To do this you need a van equipped as a grooming salon. It's worth thinking about and investigating for the future growth of your business.

You can charge $27 for a full grooming session, $5 for a comb-out, and $15 for a bath and comb-out without a haircut.

Advertise in local shopper pages, the service section of the newspaper, and by posting flyers in pet stores that do not have grooming facilities.

Personal Shopper

Start-up cost: $500 for stationery, business cards, and advertising. No equipment needed.

Break-even: Six months to a year

Annual income: $20,000 to $60,000

If you love to shop, you may have the basic skills for a from-home business. Many men and women don't have time to shop and don't enjoy it. Some people are even willing to pay someone to do it for them. Those who purchase for others are called "personal shoppers."

Many people who live in fast-paced major cities can afford a personal shopper's fees—an average of 15 to 25 percent of each article's retail price.

If becoming a personal shopper appeals to you, carefully research your city or town to assess the need. Does your area have a lot of well-paid professional people, such as doctors, lawyers, executives, bankers, or those who travel frequently? If so, you may be able to market a personal shopping service.

Look for customers through professional organizations such as business women's clubs, actors and screenwriters guilds, and civic organizations. If you add the service of wardrobe consulting, you'll gain more visibility for your business. Wardrobe consultants take inventory of a client's wardrobe and suggest what to purchase to go with and enhance the existing wardrobe. Wardrobe consultants charge up to $100 an hour.

You can advertise both services—personal shopping and wardrobe consulting—in a services directory in the newspaper. However, the best advertising will be word of mouth as your customers receive compliments for their sense of style.

Some wardrobe consultants arrange shoppers' tours to factory outlets where clients can purchase quality merchandise at reduced prices. These outings require a chartered van or bus and a plan for lunch. Since saving money is important to most people, consultants can often get coverage for their shopping events on local radio talk shows.

Consulting

Start-up cost: $500 to $2,000 for a from-home office
Break-even: Immediate to one year
Annual income: $40,000 to $200,000+

What do you know that someone would pay you to tell them? This is the essence of a consulting service and is a fairly easy from-home business to start.

A consultant's value lies in his ability to objectively evaluate a business's products, systems, or services and speak the truth about what they see. They research information helpful to a business and suggest ways to improve or streamline procedures. They usually specialize in one area and have a store of information about problems inherent to that area.

What is your expertise? Have you been a secretary or an office manager? Perhaps you could help a new company choose the right staff and the right equipment. Have you done fundraising? Perhaps you could help companies write appeal letters that bring in money. Do you have experience as a bookkeeper or accountant? Perhaps you could help clients set up their financial systems. Have you been in sales and marketing? Perhaps you could help companies increase their sales.

Whatever it is you know, somebody probably wants to know it, too. Establishing a from-home consulting service will mean making lots of contacts with businesses who might be looking for help and letting them know of your expertise. It will be easier to establish your consulting business if you are well known in a particular field and have been at it for a long time.

While you need expertise to become a consultant, you need little else but time and the ability to research answers to problems affecting a client's business. A computer, an answering machine, and a fax machine will be helpful, but you can start without them.

As always, when pricing your services, it's best to talk with others in the field. You can charge by the project or you can offer your services as an ongoing consultant on a retainer fee basis. That means you give the customer a break on the price, but you are assured a steady income.

I have several friends in the publishing industry who consult. One does magazine consulting as a supplement to her income. Another consults in all areas of publishing. He is on retainer to several large companies and says he is doing quite well.

Mall Walking

Start-up cost: $500 for business cards, stationery, and to rent a table in a mall
Break-even: Immediate to two months
Annual income: $15,000 to $30,000

Because Americans are now so health conscious, and streets can be unsafe, many people choose to walk in malls for exercise. Avia footwear company estimates there may be 500,000 mall walkers in the United States.[2] Some malls open early to accommodate mall walkers.

If this idea appeals to you, contact your local mall association and tell them what you are trying to do. Show them how your program will benefit their businesses by drawing more customers to the mall on a regular basis.

Post flyers advertising mall walks in churches, fitness centers, senior citizen clubs, hospitals, universities, and any other place where active, health-conscious people meet. Your flyer should play up the safety, comfort, convenience, and companionship of mall walking.

Another way to attract mall walkers is to set up a small portable table in the mall (clear this first with the mall owners) and load it with books and tapes on physical fitness and nutrition. Sell T-shirts and sweatshirts with your logo or a clever slogan on them.

Once your advertising efforts gain regular groups of walkers, contact health-conscious businesses in the mall and sell them a response card (a card mall walkers take back to the store for a discount) for somewhere between $200 and $300 a month. This is a form of inexpensive advertising to get mall walkers into the stores instead of just passing them by.

Print up a card with the store's name, store specialties, sale items, special discounts to walkers, and anything else the store might find helpful. Ask your mall walkers to take the cards into the stores and mention they heard about the store through the mall walkers group. It's a great arrangement: the store draws in potential health-conscious customers and you get paid to advertise the store.

A mall walking business can become a rather profitable venture. One mall-walkers group in Florida recruited sixty merchants to participate in their mall-walk venture. Each merchant paid $250 per month to advertise his store. That paid the mall-walk organizer $15,000 gross income per month. The group's only expenses were printing the cards for store owners and printing flyers to recruit mall walkers.

Depending on the need and the number of hours you want to work, you can lead walks every couple of hours or just a couple of hours a day.

Seminar Planner
  Start-up cost: $3,000 for computer and software
  Break-even: After one event
  Annual income: $50,000 to $200,000

In an information age, people will gladly pay for good information. Individuals who attend seminars pay anywhere from $250 to $500 for a single day's class, and some promoters make up to $1 million a year holding seminars.

The secret to successful seminars is to pack them with information on a carefully niched topic. For example: A seminar on printing might include information about paper, layout and design, what to include in a design, what to avoid, and new techniques that add splash and dash for little money.

Suppose the idea of holding seminars appeals to you but you don't have expertise on any subject. Find someone who does and become his or her promoter. You could then conduct several seminars at one time and increase your income without carrying the full responsibility for the conference. You would take a percentage of the total income.

Seminars are held in hotel conference rooms, gymnasiums, and convention centers. They have to be well advertised—a major expense that varies from hotel to hotel. Costs for printing the flyer, postage, and the rental of names can cost several thousand dollars. Rental of a hotel conference room can cost between $800 and $1,000 for one day. Sometimes, if the conference is a two-day event and attendees choose to stay in the hotel, the conference room is free.

To determine what to charge, observe what others are charging for a seminar, add up your expenses, determine what your time is worth, then charge accordingly. (This process can also reveal if seminar planning is feasible for you.)

Special Interest Swap Meets
Start-up cost: $500
Break-even: One or two events
Annual income: $30,000

Consider a home business that organizes special interest swap meets. The people you draw would be intensely interested in your specialty and would be more likely to buy than those who attend all-purpose swap meets.

Your main from-home job is to promote the meet by finding the sellers and letting buyers know about the event. Your income results from contracting the booth space (which probably will only be a table space) and by placing ads in special interest publications. You can charge anywhere from $25 to $100 for each space.

Let's say your special interest is watches. Look in the yellow pages and contact every watchmaker and repairer within a two-hundred-mile radius to tell them about your swap-meet idea. Antiques dealers might also be interested if they have enough watches (perhaps even clocks) to warrant attendance at your swap meet. Don't forget to contact wholesalers of watches to see if they'd like to participate.

Because you have a small specialty item, you wouldn't need to hold the swap meet in a large parking lot. Why not use a room at a hotel in a centralized location?

You can draw customers by posting flyers in related businesses or distributing them in parking lots, especially in the area where the sale will be held.

It is appropriate to charge swap meet attendees a small entry fee of fifty cents to a dollar. The entrance fee will help defray some of your advertising expenses. If you conduct a specialty swap meet a couple times a year, you will soon build customer loyalty from people who are interested in your specialty.

Airport Shuttle
Start-up cost: $500 for business cards, advertising, and magnetic signs (This assumes you already have an appropriate vehicle)
Break-even: One month
Annual income: $50,000 to $80,000

Thousands of people fly all over the country for business and recreational purposes. Most of them hate the idea of leaving their cars in airport parking lots. They also hate the cost of cab fare or limo service.

Your from-home shuttle business can eliminate all the hassles for your passengers. Many people would use a shuttle service that picked them up at home, loaded their bags, and delivered them to their terminals for a nominal price.

If you're thinking of this kind of from-home work, check into your state's qualifications for a driver's license. Be sure you are carrying adequate insurance of the proper kind, and investigate whether you need to be bonded.

To let people know what you are doing, get a couple of magnetic signs for each side of your car—it's inexpensive advertising and provides recognition for your customers.

To set your fees, consider to and from airport fuel consumption, insurance, wear and tear on your car, and then add a sizable profit for yourself. Charge by the one-way trip with a discount for a round-trip fare.

Handyman
Start-up cost: $1,200 to $1,500
Break-even: Two to three months
Annual income: $40,000 to $65,000

If you know how to fix things, you probably already have a shelf full of tools. Why not use them to earn money fixing things for others—window blinds, simple plumbing projects, doors that stick, broken window panes, broken fences, simple electrical problems, broken tiles, small appliances, electrical plugs, and much more.

Lots of homeowners would love to hire a handyman with diverse skills who charges a reasonable rate of $15-$25 an hour.

Check into community regulations before you launch your from-home handyman business. You may need certain licenses and you should carry liability insurance. Once you get going, you should be able to pick up customers easily. List yourself in the service section of the newspaper and get yourself an answering machine or service to take calls while you're out on a job.

Child Shuttle Service
Start-up cost: $15,000 to $20,000 for a van, advertising, and business cards; $500 for advertising and a pair of magnetic signs if you don't need to buy a van.
Break-even: Six months to one year
Annual income: $40,000 to $65,000

Just recently I heard about a woman in the Denver area who shuttles kids to and from events for working parents. A visitor standing on a street corner saw the van go by. The idea intrigued her, so she went home to Boise, found a partner, and established her own child-transportation company.

With more working parents than ever before, this is a viable business to consider. Parents don't like to leave their kids standing at the bus stop when they leave for work in the morning, and they can't always get free of work obligations to take children to ballet lessons and soccer practice.

A couple of caveats: Hours for this business are long (children must be transported to school early in the morning and picked up after their activities in the evening), and you need to be able to climb in and out of the van as many times as needed (kids need to be escorted to and from their doors).

If you're thinking about this kind of from-home work, be sure to check with a lawyer and the state motor vehicle department about regulations for transporting passengers and the required liability insurance. You'll also need a background check by the FBI and the state, and you'll need to acquire taxi-type insurance and answer questions about licensing. Since this is a fairly new idea, it may take time to establish, but you can be thankful others are already paving the way.

Even though school transportation is a big part of this business, it is not seasonal, since kids need to go places all year long.

Window Washing
Start-up cost: $200-$300 for flyers, small ad in newspaper, ladder, and squeegees
Break-even: Immediately to one month
Annual income: $45,000 to $60,000

If I could find someone to wash my twenty-seven windows at a reasonable price, I'd have the windows washed several times a year. There's a lucrative business out there for someone who doesn't mind washing windows. If that's you, think about the limits as to what you will and won't do. Be sure you know how to wash windows without leaving streaks or you'll find yourself doing the job over. You'll need:

- lots of rags
- cleaning compounds
- squeegees
- perhaps a power washer
- ladders of a couple of different heights

Run a small ad in the service section of the newspaper, post brightly-colored posters in grocery stores, or tuck flyers under windshield wiper blades. This business probably works best at the change of seasons—winter to spring and summer to fall.

Find out what the locals are charging for window washing and charge a little less. If you're good, and available to work with your customers' time schedules, you'll quickly make up the difference in earnings.

Security Patrol Service
Start-up cost: $500 for magnetic signs, advertising
Break-even: One month
Annual income: $24,000 to $36,000

This is a private service where a patrol car cruises through a certain neighborhood or neighborhoods to keep an eye on things. The presence of such a patrol car is perceived as a deterrent to crime.

A security patrol service can also pick up mail and newspapers for customers away on vacations and try windows and doors to make sure they are locked. An additional service could be the sale of security systems, deadbolts, window locks, and other security devices.

In case of an emergency, the patrol service's rapid and efficient communication with the local police is essential. They'll take it from there and be thankful you alerted them. False alarms will cause the police to think you are less than reliable, so be sure the emergency is genuine.

Fees vary and a little investigation of other companies in your area would be the best way to determine them. Some companies are netting as much as $100,000 a year. In a time of high-crime, high-burglary rates, there's room for another security company. The only equipment you need is a car, an emergency light, and a cellular phone.

Service Broker
Start-up cost: $3,000 for computer and database software
Break-even: Two to three months
Annual income: $40,000 to $60,000

Service brokering simply means you become the liaison between people who have a service to offer and the person who needs the service. You charge those you are brokering a percentage—usually about 25 percent.

You can broker any kind of service, even if you don't know much about the service. All you need is a good phone manner, some organizational skills, and a little marketing ability. If you have a computer with a database program, all the better.

To get started, check the yellow pages and newspaper ads. Call all the services listed. Find out who does handyman repair work, hauls trash, remodels houses, sets type, proofreads, transports the elderly, is a personal shopper, and so on. Offer to refer their services to customers. Charge them a small monthly retainer fee or work out a commission for each referral. It's a win-win situation for everyone.

Before you broker any service, get to know the independent contractors. Ask for references and check out their work with previous customers. Visit their places of business. Compare their rates with those of their competitors. Make sure you are recommending someone who does quality work. Your success as a broker will depend on it.

You can build a database of clients to broker by listing them in your computer or in a card file. A client entry might look something like this:

THE ABC YARD SERVICE
123 Sunnyside Street
Yourtown, Ohio

Services provided:

Mowing	Deep watering
Fertilizing	Plantings
Weeding	Tree spraying

Fees:
Mowing—$20 weekly
Fertilizing—$50 twice a year
Weeding—$15 per hour

Availability: Daily, Monday-Saturday

Method of payment: Cash, check. No credit cards, please.

Once you have an active database of committed service organizations to broker, you're ready to advertise. Advertising does not have to be expensive. You can put up flyers in grocery stores and laundromats or leave them on car windows. You can put a small display ad in the service section of the paper or phone directory. A highly effective method of advertising is frequent radio advertising; if people hear something enough, it sinks in. If you can't afford radio advertising, make it a goal as your from-home business grows.

You can broker a specialized service or a broad base of service businesses. Whatever you decide, you need to know this is not a spare-time business. Once people understand what you are doing, you can expect calls at all times of the day or evening—whenever someone has a problem and needs help.

Check with your attorney and your insurance agent to see what the liability would be for brokering a firm that might do an inferior job. That's the downside. The up side is having a business that makes money and helps people.

Here is a partial list of firms to broker:

Restaurants, specialty food shops, caterers—know their food specialties and services

Theaters—what's playing where

Major stores—what the sales are on any day

Museums and galleries—hours they are open, traveling exhibits

Limousine Service—who they are, how much they charge

Doctors, Dentists, Veterinarians, Emergency Care

Attorneys and their specialties

Accountants—prices for various services

Private schools, classes, other kinds of lessons

Landscape, tree, and gardening services

Hauling land cleanup services

Moving services—which ones do specialty (such as pianos) and other heavy moving

Cleaning services

Personal shopper services

Remodeling, carpentry, and electrical services

Pet care services

Child and elderly care services

Florists

Home decorators

LOTS OF OTHER IDEAS

Aerobic Instructor. Requires easily attainable expertise.

Animal breeding. Requires some research, patience, and a couple of good animals.

Assembly work. Be careful to find a reputable firm that pays commensurate with the amount of work you do. Some ads falsely promise mega bucks.

Baby-sitting and other in-home child care. Requires a love of children, patience, and following state, county, and city rules with regard to child care.

Baking for local restaurants. Requires a love of baking and a willingness to make the contacts. Check into health ordinances and city health laws.

Barter service. Requires some means of matching those who want to barter goods or services.

Bicycle repair. Minimal equipment needed, but some easily attainable expertise. Practice on your own bikes first.

Candle-making. Could be a specialty item—certain colors or incorporating an announcement or trinket.

Children's birthday party organizer. Lots of people would be happy to pay for this.

Cleaning and janitorial services.

Clipping service. Clip newspaper and magazine articles for research and information companies.

Clowning for birthday parties and other special events. This is different from planning the parties.

Deliverer of court papers. Somebody has to transport important documents around a city. Some of these are court documents but others might be for banks and businesses.

Dog walking. Americans are tied to their pets, even if they live in city apartments. Have you seen them—the dog walkers? Usually they have three or four pooches on leashes, leading them around the park.

Envelope addressing and stuffing. Find out if you're expected to pay for any part of the expense of mailing and, if so, how you will be reimbursed.

Etiquette counseling. Corporations will pay you to teach employees the ins and outs of business etiquette. One etiquette counselor charges $1,500 for a twelve-hour course. Students could include schools, churches, and even individual families.

Garage sale planner and promoter. Requires almost no equipment and only a little experience. Watch the "For Sale" signs in your town. Those people will be moving soon and you can almost bet they'll want to have a garage sale before they go. Knock on their door, hand them your flyer, and tell them you'll organize and run their garage sale for a fee or percentage.

Hair care. Cutting and all other beauty services. You need a cosmetologist's license before you start cutting or coloring someone's hair. And check city zoning ordinances for hair care in your home.

Herb gardener and seller. Herbs are the one plant that almost thrive on neglect: If you overfertilize and overwater herbs they are not as tasty. The whole area of herb culture and usage is at the highest point since colonial settlers used herbs for medicines because they had nothing else. Once again people are looking to herbs for medicinal purposes as well as food seasoning. Herb gardening requires a plot of ground, a few packets of seeds, and some creativity in how to sell the herbs you grow. Herb gardens are popular places for weekend gardeners to visit. Why not set up an herb tea garden and serve herb teas and pastries?

Housecleaning. Minimal equipment needed and you probably have all the skills you need. You might talk to some professional housecleaners and learn their shortcuts. The faster you work the more houses you can clean and the more money you can make. Don't overlook new construction housecleaning. It pays well.

House-sitting service. Charge a finder's fee to the person needing the house sitter and you'll never have to leave your from-home office.

Image consulting. Millions of people want to improve their personal appearance but don't know how to do it. You can make money teaching people how to look and feel better about themselves, whether for business, performance appearances, or just day-to-day image. I was once helped by a workshop leader who gave points on what to wear and not to wear for a television appearance. There is no exam to become an image consultant. However, many consultants have been involved in the fashion industry. And there are schools throughout the country that offer courses in image consulting. Image consulting covers hair, skin, makeup, and wardrobe consulting, and may include teaching poise, manners, and what to do in specific business situations. Image consultants don't work for small change. Some are grossing from $100,000 to $200,000 a year.

Lawn care. This can be a very labor-intensive way to make a living. Maybe you'd just like to mow the lawns. Maybe you'd just like to keep flowers in the planters all summer long. Decide which part of lawn care you'd like to do and how hard you want to work at it.

Pet-sitting. The combination of Americans' love of pets and love of travel creates a ready-made business. You'll need an area to keep other people's pets, unless you plan to just take them into your home as part of your family. In some cases pet-sitting may mean going to a client's home and putting out food for an animal.

Toy making and repair. There's a great market for homemade toys. Closely following this is the repair of used toys for resale. You can buy used toys from garage sales, thrift shops, and resale shops. I often see women buying old dolls by the armloads in these places. They fix the hair, repaint the faces, and make new clothes. Then the dolls are ready to be sold at craft shows and fairs.

Tutoring. Here's from-home work that pays big dividends in satisfaction. Not only do you earn money for helping a child or adult learn, you have the pleasure of giving that person a lifelong gift.

Vegetable grower and seller. If you love to grow things and have the space, this is a great from-home work idea. Sell what you produce at farmer's markets, roadside stands, or by advertising under "Good Things to Eat" in the paper.

Wedding consultant. People just keep getting married, and they need help to do it right. Before you launch out as a full-fledged wedding consultant, you might want to volunteer to help someone who is already established.

These are only a few ideas for home-based businesses; let your imagination come up with many more ideas. If you can find a need and figure out how to fill it, you will succeed.

CHAPTER FOUR

From-Home Work Ideas That Require Equipment

Sometimes a simple piece of equipment is all it takes to start a from-home business. Here's a case in point. A young woman decided to buy a stereo system. Her parents felt that if she wanted the stereo, she had to earn the money to pay for it. So, she bought a badge-making machine—you know, those big buttons that advertise something or have a clever slogan on them.

Then she contacted businesses and organizations in her area and set about making badges for them. It wasn't long until she had enough money for the stereo system.

Her initial investment was $40 for the machine and beginning supplies. Of course, before she could begin making a profit she had to pay back that initial investment, which she did with the first order. Customers provided printed or visual material; her part of the process was to turn their printed material into a badge.

Let's look at badge-making and some other from-home businesses that use simple equipment you may already have or can buy at a minimal investment.

Badge-Making

Start-up cost: $29.95 for machine, $.25 per blank badge
Break-even: One month. Charge $1.50 for each finished badge
Annual income: If you made 100 badges five nights a week you would earn about $30,000 in a year

Brainstorm for a minute the things you could put on badges. Besides the obvious—advertising businesses and political campaigns—here are some other applications.

- Show a newborn baby's picture to be sent instead of a traditional birth announcement.
- Promote an author and his book. An author could wear a button with a picture of his new book or the words, "Ask me about my new book." Publishing companies often have buttons made to advertise books and authors at trade shows.
- Ask the question, "How am I doing?" and add a chain food store's logo.
- Encourage safety for kids. Sell to both private and public schools.
- Display a big question mark for any information-based service company.

If you decide badge-making might be a good business for you, buy a machine, jot down your ideas, keep your eyes open for existing ideas (you don't always have to reinvent the wheel), and approach companies and businesses about how they could use an advertising badge.

Balloon Gift-Wrapping Machine

Start-up cost: $1,500 for machine, video, phone support, business cards, mall and flea market fees, business license

Break-even: Two to four months—you'll need to sell 250 balloons to pay back your investment

Annual income: $15,000 as a part-time job

You can capitalize on people's inclination to procrastinate about gift buying. Say it's 3:00 P.M., and Linda Sue has to go to a dinner birthday celebration for a favorite aunt. She's still at her desk, with no time to shop. What should she do? She should call your balloon gift-wrapping business. Gifts presented inside a balloon have unique appeal.

Besides the initial outlay of money for the balloon-inflating machine, there is the ongoing cost of balloons, ribbons, and small gift items. Balloons cost about $1 each and the stuffed balloons sell for about $6.50 each, depending on what you've put inside. That's a pretty good profit.

By taking your machine to a mall just before a holiday such as Valentine's Day, Easter, or Christmas, you should be able to pay back your initial investment in a couple of days, even after paying mall fees. Flea markets and craft shows are also great places to set up for business.

To increase sales, have a small stock of stuffed animals, soaps, toys, and other gift items. Then you can either balloon-wrap your customers' prepurchased gifts or provide the whole package. Decorate your table or booth with ready-to-go gift items already encased in balloons for those impulse buyers who come by your booth.

One of the best things about a balloon-wrap operation is that it can be performed by people with back problems or other physical disabilities, since it requires only the use of the hands. And it is a low-stress job. If a balloon breaks, so what? It's just a balloon. Get another one and try again.

Be aware this is not easy money. There are key times when a lot of money can be made—at fairs and around the holidays. But there are a lot of times when you will set up at a craft show and sell little. To extend your business, hand out business cards to all customers and prospective customers at these events. Contact businesses, florists, and gift stores offering to balloon-wrap their customers' purchases. Advertise in the yellow pages and local newspapers and magazines.

There are several companies with balloon gift-wrapping machines with different costs and requirements for setting up.

One is Balloon Wrap, 18032 Lemon Dr., #C-144, Yorba Linda, California 92686, (714) 993-2295. This company has two thousand dealers scattered throughout the country and in thirty other countries. The owners claim that about 80 percent of their dealers are home-based.

Repairing Cracked Windshields
Start-up cost: $1,500 for equipment and advertising
Break-even: Two to four months
Annual income: $40,000 to $60,000

If there's anything you can count on, it's a ding in a windshield several times during the life of your car. Insurance companies will pay the total amount to have a windshield chip repaired rather than replace the windshield.

There's room for a from-home business operator to do this lucrative work. All you need is the tool for making these repairs and the training, and there will be plenty of business. One company, Glas-Weld Systems, Inc., will train you and provide the necessary tool for $1,200. This is not a franchise business. To reach them call 1-800-321-2597 and meet some really nice folks.

Upholsterer
Start-up cost: $2,500 for a commercial sewing machine. You'll need a vehicle to transport furniture (could be rented in the beginning)
Break-even: Six months to one year
Annual income: $30,000 to $40,000

Besides the commercial sewing machine, upholstering requires only a few tools, a space for some very messy work, and some basic knowledge, which can be acquired through courses at a technical school, home study (there are some good, easy-to-understand books), or adult education courses. Upholstering is not difficult to learn and requires more tacking and gluing than sewing. The tools you need besides a commercial sewing machine are:

- A tool to cut foam rubber (unless you have it cut to size at an upholstery shop)
- Tack hammers
- Tools for pulling staples and tearing the furniture apart before beginning the upholstery process
- A web stretcher
- A good pair of heavy-duty scissors

By the time you've redone several of your own pieces of furniture, you'll be ready to hang out your shingle and start doing it for others.

Advertising can be a small ad in local newspapers, flyers tacked up in grocery stores, business cards handed out to friends, decorators, and furniture repair people, and word-of-mouth from satisfied customers.

Chimney Sweep

Start-up cost: $1,000 for tools, ladders, advertising, licenses, and insurance
Break-even: Two to three months
Annual income: $40,000

If you're not afraid to climb up on a roof and you have a good insurance plan, this might be a business for you. With the oil crisis a few years ago came the return of wood burning as a source of heat. With that came the need for chimney sweeps.

The only equipment you would need are a few brushes, a couple of ladders, a couple of tarps to protect the customer's floors (and perhaps a top hat and tails for effect!), and you're off to earn money.

A sweep job should take no more than an hour and a half and you can charge $50 to $75 per chimney. You should be able to do five or six jobs a day.

Christmas Tree Sales

Start-up cost: $11,000 for trees, fencing for lot (optional), saws, pruners
Break-even: One week
Annual income: $4,000 to $8,000 (part time, once a year)

If you're looking for a once-a-year, high-profit enterprise, consider a Christmas tree lot. The markup on Christmas trees is about 200 to 300 percent. Most small lot operators walk away with a $5,000 to $8,000 profit for about a month's worth of work.

A downside to this business is that Christmas tree lots have to be open at the busiest time of the year. A lot operator needs to be in attendance from early morning until late at night in sometimes inclement weather.

You'll need a couple of saws and pruners and a place to keep warm. It's also going to cost about $10,000 for a stock of about 700 trees.

Set up in a good residential neighborhood, and if it works, set up every year in the same place for return customers. This can be a profitable family enterprise and a lot of fun as well.

Gift-Wrapping Service

Start-up cost: $500 for table, wrapping paper, ribbons, and other accessories

Break-even: One month

Annual income: $2,000 to $7,000. Can be seasonal as a part-time job close to holidays

You'll need a table or a cart, lots of beautiful paper, ribbons, and other gift attachments, scissors, and some good ideas.

This idea works best seasonally. If you only want to do from-home work a few weeks of the year, this would be perfect. Set up a table (with permission and having paid the fees) in a mall or shopping center.

Develop a standard, deluxe, and extra-deluxe wrap and charge accordingly. Check local department stores' gift-wrapping departments to see what they charge for various sized packages.

Janitorial Service

Start-up cost: $2,500 to $5,000 for cleaning compounds, cleaning machines (rent them at first), and other cleaning supplies, plus advertising and business forms

Break-even: Two to six months

Annual income: $25,000 to $50,000

We all run on different internal time clocks. Some of us are morning larks and some of us are night owls. Here's a job for a night owl. Most janitorial services are performed after businesses close, so it's a great idea for those who like to sleep late in the mornings. Some people hang on to their day jobs while establishing their cleaning business.

Every church, office building, school, and health care facility has to be cleaned by someone, and that someone could be you. Start by contacting businesses within a ten-mile radius of your home. Try to get a cleaning contract with someone. Approach businesses that big cleaning companies overlook. Add some nontraditional cleaning tasks such as windows and upholstery, rug dyeing, ceiling cleaning, and parking lot maintenance. When you're driving around, look for new office buildings and contact the management. Find out if there are items in the building that require special treatment, such as Berber carpets, then find out how to care for those items and make a professional cleaning presentation that offers your expertise.

Most janitorial contractors charge by the square foot. You'll have to call some cleaning agencies in your area to determine what the going rate is for your city.

Check out this magazine for cleaners: *Cleaning Business*, 1512 Western Ave., P.O. Box 1273, Seattle, WA 98111. The subscription rate is twenty dollars.

Professional Tool and Saw Sharpening
Start-up cost: $500 to $1500 for grinders, files, rotary files and machines to set angle of teeth
Break-even: One to two months
Annual income: $8 to $10 per hour to equal $15,000 to $20,000

When I was a little girl, traveling men would come to the door of our house and ask if we had tools to sharpen. We always did.

Good tools deserve care, and sharpening them regularly is important. But where does one go to have a hand saw or a pair of scissors or garden shears sharpened? Where do you go to have knives sharpened? There are places, but they are tough to find and are usually an aside to another business.

Dressmaking shears can be sharpened in a fabric store, but they are sent out to some from-home business person. Why not go directly to the business person? Saws are sharpened as a sideline in hardware and tool stores, but usually you must wait for someone to come in and do the job.

If you think you could be a tool sharpener, you'll need a grinder, some files, and whetstones. Good advertising is a must. Why not set up in a shopping center or even a grocery store once a month and see the long line form for this needed service.

Snow Removal

Start-up cost: $10 for a snow shovel to $2,000 for a snow blower

Break-even: One to two months in snow season

Annual income: $10,000 to $30,000 for seasonal work

It's a helpless feeling to wake up to fifteen inches of snow in your driveway. Snow removal is seasonal but essential.

My snow removal person comes to remove the snow from my walk and driveway any time it's deeper than four inches. His four-wheel drive pickup truck has a plow attached to the front. He charges $15 to clear my fifty-foot driveway.

Snow can also be removed with a shovel. Many a young entrepreneur got his start with a snow shovel. Snow also can be removed with a snow blowing machine and, of course, with a plow attached to a truck.

To determine your fee, research how much your competitors are charging and set yours at the low end or in the middle.

T-Shirt Decorating
>   **Start-up cost:** $1,000 to $2,000 for heat-seal machine,
>   transfers, T-shirts in various colors and sizes, advertising
>   **Break-even:** Two to three months
>   **Annual income:** $20,000 to $35,000. Excellent for part-
>   time or extra income

It looks like picture-message T-shirts are here to stay. And customized T-shirts are very popular. To get into this business you need a heat-seal press and time and temperature controls. A machine will cost around $500.

To operate a decorative T-shirt shop out of your home, you will need to advertise widely to get your business started. Put a magnetic sign on your car; post a flyer in local markets showing your best T-shirts; set up for special occasions in malls, trade shows, flea markets, or other places a lot of people gather. You could set up on weekends only and in short order repay your initial investment.

Besides the heat-seal machine, you'll need an assortment of T-shirts and designs that you can purchase wholesale. If you can find a niche or specialty, all the better for your sales.

Refinishing Furniture
>   **Start-up cost:** $500 for stripping compound, sandpaper,
>   finishing compounds, business cards, and advertising
>   **Break-even:** Immediate to two months
>   **Annual income:** $40,000 to $50,000

Good furniture costs a lot of money and people think twice about getting rid of it. Done on a small scale, furniture refinishing makes a great from-home business. Done on a large scale—high volume—you will probably need a stripping tank.

There are people who don't want their furniture dip-stripped since it is very hard on the wood and raises the grain. They would prefer hand stripping, which means gently removing the finish, sanding, filling holes, and applying a new finish.

Tools for this operation are various kinds of scrapers and picks for getting the old finish out of crevices, sanding devices, and rags and paint brushes for applying stains and sealers. Finding a good location is also important: when done indoors, stripping furniture requires good ventilation. Because the chemicals used in strippers don't respond well to the cold, working outside may not always be a good choice.

By taking the idea a step further you could become the restorer of antique furniture. This specialty craft requires training. The best way to get that training is to work with a qualified restorer as an apprentice. It could take two to four years to learn the craft, because it is easy to devalue a piece by applying the wrong material or finish. Done correctly, your work could increase the value and make the piece more serviceable. Besides, you get to work on a piece of history. You get to put your hands on a handcrafted piece that has been in existence for hundreds of years and repair it so that it will exist for many more years.

Advertise by displaying before and after pieces at antique shows. As in all businesses, the very best advertising is word of mouth by satisfied customers. After you've done a few pieces successfully, you'll be in demand as a restorer of antiques or refinisher of furniture.

Carpet Cleaning

Start-up cost: $3,000 to $4,000 for your own equipment, or rent equipment to start. You will need a station wagon or a van to haul the heavy carpet cleaning equipment.
Break-even: Six months to a year
Annual income: $30,000 to $50,000

Carpet cleaning is not complicated. All you need is a carpet-cleaning machine of some kind. In the beginning the machine can be quite simple. As time goes on you could exchange it for something as sophisticated as a truck that heats its own water and generates its own power. For the most part, and especially in the beginning, use the customer's power and hot water. What you are providing is service.

You'll need to learn about spot removal methods and products and professional steam-cleaning machines. As you build a customer base and do a good job, you should be able to return a couple of times a year to the same house or business. Start by cleaning friends' carpets and the offices of people you know to get word-of-mouth advertising going. Advertise in local papers, the yellow pages, and on bulletin boards. You might even call twenty or thirty people from the phone book each evening for contacts.

You should be able to gross about $12 to $15 per hour, or you can charge $.10 to $.25 per square foot. Ongoing expenses are cleaning products, gasoline to get you to the site, and upkeep on the equipment. If you do only five or six jobs a week you should be able to net around $500 to $600 per week. If you do two or three jobs a day, you'll net $1,000-$1,800 a week.

Radon Detection

Start-up cost: $500 for canisters, lab fees, business cards, and advertising
Break-even: Two months
Annual income: $10,000 (part time)

Radon is a colorless, odorless gas that results from the breakdown of uranium in the earth's surface. It has been known to cause lung cancer and it can accumulate at unhealthy levels in homes. It is in the soil everywhere, but more prevalent in some areas of the country.

In Colorado, radon testing is required on land before a

home is built. Someone has to do that testing. The simplest way to become a radon tester is to buy the test kits wholesale from a reliable lab. Usually the kit is a charcoal-filled canister, which is placed in a client's home for a few days. You place it, pick it up, send it to the lab, and give the results to your client. There is no expertise required, as the lab does all the testing. This would make a great part-time job or a way to supplement existing income.

Work with real estate agents, advertise in the yellow pages, and contact homeowners who have never had their homes tested.

Investigate what others are asking for the service and charge accordingly. Canisters cost around $10, including lab work. The largest expense will be advertising.

"FOOD, GLORIOUS FOOD"

So goes the line from the musical *Oliver.* There are so many food-related, from-home ideas that food deserves a section all by itself. Depending on the uniqueness, quality, and presentation of your food items, you could do very well. After all, that's how Debbi Fields (Mrs. Fields Cookies) got her start.

Another woman who has yet to achieve the fame of Debbi Fields lives in Cambridge, Vermont. Peggy Myott bakes Dutch apple muffins, sour dough carrot cakes, chocolate cakes, brownies, and Congo bars from an oven in a woodshed behind her house. She also bakes bread, sour cream and buttermilk donuts, and loads of rolls and cinnamon buns dripping with caramelized sugar. She loves her work and sells her products through local grocery stores to add cash to the family coffer.[1]

To enter this type of from-home business, you only need a dough mixer, an oven, some bowls and measuring devices, and a way to package what you produce. You also need a great idea. What family recipe do friends and family beg you to make? What do you cook better than anyone else? Have you tried making and selling something, perhaps for a charitable bake sale, and found it a smashing success?

I love to make jelly and jam. It's one of the easiest things to do, and the results are so satisfying. When I moved to Colorado I saw fruit on some low bushes and remembered from my childhood what they were—chokecherries. Now, there's a reason why they are called chokecherries. They are the most mouth-puckering fruit around, but they make wonderful, almost grape-flavored red jelly. So, I gathered fruit and made some jelly and then took a jar to the office. It didn't last long.

One of my colleagues wanted to make some, so I described the process. Shortly after that I went on vacation and left him to manufacture his own jelly. When I called home to check my messages, he'd left an urgent plea, "Help, something's gone wrong with my jelly." Since my vacation was nearly over, I waited until I came home. My first morning in the office, Tom came to me, got down on one knee, and said, "Oh, thou great jelly guru." I decided then that if jelly-making were what I wanted to do, I could become a manufacturer of jellies with chokecherry jelly as my specialty.

What great food ideas do you have that people can't resist? Let's see what some others have done.

Food-Crafting

Start-up cost: $200 for special kitchen utensils such as melon ball scoops, lemon zesters, paring knives, coring devices, etc.

Break-even: Immediate to two months

Annual income: $10,000 to $20,000. This would make a great part-time or supplemental income job.

Can you make a fruit basket from a melon? Flowers from carrots and radishes? If you have a flair for making food look spectacular, you can prepare items for special events like weddings, bar mitzvahs, office parties, and receptions.

There are a couple of ways you can turn your talent into cash. One is to contact caterers, cooks, and gourmet restaurants whose main task is the preparation of food but who need decorative food items to enhance their food. Radish roses, carrot curls, turnips cut into floral shapes, melon baskets, and many other imaginative uses of fruits and vegetables take time yet are often the touches that transform the plain into the festive. Don't forget the use of edible flowers and herbs as decorative items. Offer your services, and if you have skill, caterers and cooks will become regular customers.

You can also make money from food crafting by teaching classes in your home or through local recreation programs or community college programs.

Catering

Start-up cost: $1,000 to $80,000—if you have to install a professional kitchen. You may need to purchase serving pieces and tableware, depending on how extensive you wish to make your operation.

Break-even: One month to three years

Annual income: $50,000 to $100,000

Outlay for equipment of a full catering service can be expensive, but it is not necessary to begin on such a large scale. Start small and build. For example, you could start with a dessert service or do relish trays or meats and cheeses trays for office functions and receptions. You could do afternoon teas for fashion shows or in-home gatherings of ladies, or you could plan, cook, and serve small dinner parties in homes. These intimate little gatherings are "in" and those who provide food for them are well paid. The beauty of this kind of catering is that you can control how much you want to do and what kind of catering appeals to you.

A different way to advertise than the usual channels is to stage a party to celebrate your grand opening and invite prospective customers. Hand out business cards and flyers with menus and choices of food and parties. Become known for something special such as great cheesecake, Yorkshire pudding and roast beef, or marvelous, melt-in-your-mouth tea cakes. Use ice sculptures or extraordinary table settings.

Cake Making and Decorating

Start-up cost: $500 for pans, ingredients, advertising
Break-even: One to two months
Annual income: $35,000 if you do twenty cakes a week

Birthdays, showers, and weddings are occasions that demand very special cakes. All you need besides your mixer and stove are cake pans in various shapes and sizes and cake decorating tools. You may already have a knack for decorating cakes, but if not, a few hours in a cake decorating class should give you the skills you need.

To get word-of-mouth advertising started, send a decorated cake to school with your child, contribute a decorated cake to a bake sale, volunteer to be the cake baker for a family member's office party. Send along a business card listing your specialties and it won't be long before you receive business.

Make a trip to a bakery to learn how much you can charge for a cake. Even though bakery cakes often lack the creativity and taste of homemade, they are still expensive.

Just to give you an idea what to charge, one cake decorator charges $13 for an 8-inch one layer cake and $15 for a two-layer cake. An 11-by-15-inch sheet cake is $25. A 12-by-18-inch cake is $35. You will have to make some calls and do some investigation for charges in your area.

When you get some expertise, you can teach classes through adult education and local recreational programs. Even if you don't make much by teaching, it's a great way to advertise your business.

Home Canning

Start-up cost: $200 for a pressure cooker and canning kettle, an automatic food chopper, canning jars, measuring cups, a timer, a jar lifter, a funnel and pot holders
Break-even: Immediate to one month
Annual income: $30,000 to $40,000 for full time. Can be done part time or for supplemental income

Everyone seems to be interested in foods without preservatives. And with the wave of nostalgia over things past and a desire for "real"-tasting foods, home canning is back. But for those who don't have the time, this is where you come in.

You'll need a good pressure cooker and a supply of canning jars and lids. It's vitally important to learn how to can. Improperly home-canned food can be lethal, but properly canned food is delicious and satisfying to the palate. Learn by reading cookbooks and manuals, especially those which come with the pressure cooker. Don't take shortcuts. Follow times and pressures exactly. You can also learn from people who have always home canned—your mother or an aunt, for example. Remember that the end product will only be as good as the produce you use. Look for the best and tastiest fruits and vegetables available.

When you learn the skill of home canning, you will also be able to teach classes on the subject. In the winter months, when there's little or nothing to can, get involved with a local recreation or college extension program and teach. These programs set the fees and you will receive an honorarium. But if you conduct your own classes, charge $25 to $35 for a one-day training session. Add to your income by buying good canning manuals at wholesale and reselling them to the class, or, better yet, write your own canning manual and sell it.

Think about specialty items that would have great appeal to customers. How about pickled crab apples, watermelon pickles, salsa, peaches or pickled peaches, or mincemeat for pies?

You can sell your product by taking orders and filling them, selling to someone with a gift basket business, selling to specialty shops, or setting up stands at malls, flea markets, or other high-traffic areas.

One of the beauties of home-food production is that it can be done anywhere you live. One woman was married to a naval officer and lived in a number of places. She continued to manufacture food products and to send her product list to her mail-order customers from wherever she happened to live. It worked well for her. Today she runs a million-dollar gourmet food business.[2]

Jams and Jellies

Start-up cost: $200 for a jam kettle, fruit mill, jelly bag, funnel, and jelly glasses or jars
Break-even: One to two months
Annual income: $10,000 to $40,000 full time. Can be done part time or for supplemental income

Homemade jams and jellies have great appeal and can be sold to specialty shops and fine food markets. Find something unique to make, such as mint jelly, hot-pepper jelly, or tomato preserves. Perhaps you could specialize in jellies and jams made from wild fruit if you have an abundant supply. Many people have started their profitable from-home work situation by getting out the jelly-making kettle. One of those was Cordelia Knott of Knott's Berry Farm fame. She made her first strawberry jams at home and now they can be found on the shelves of supermarkets all across the country.

Only simple equipment is needed: a big kettle, a food mill for grinding fruit, a jelly sack for straining out seeds and providing a clear juice for the jelly, jars, and lids. You might search for unique jelly jars or decorate the tops with fabric or ribbons to give them your own highly identifiable look on the grocery store shelf.

At first, advertising can be by word of mouth, at craft fairs, flea markets, and malls. When you exhibit your wares, offer samples. You can also post flyers and advertise in local papers. You might even borrow Christmas lists from friends who love your jellies and jams.

To determine what to charge, figure all your costs and then multiply the result by four. Check the price of commercial jellies and jams to see if you are pricing yourself out of the market. Charge as much as you can and still be competitive.

Think about selling a variety box of jellies and jams. That means finding boxes or baskets to hold the assortment. Such a package would, however, help you to sell a lot more product in one place at a good price point—$25 to $100.

Coffee Room

Start-up cost: $1,000 to $5,000 to outfit a room as a coffee shop and to buy an espresso machine, coffee cups, paper supplies—coffee cups, plates for pastries, napkins, etc.
Break-even: Six months to one year
Annual income: $25,000 to $60,000

If you live in a high traffic area, such as a city, you can take a room of your home, your patio, or garage and convert it into a coffee room. But you'll have to think of a way to make yours stand out from all the other coffee bars.

There are several ways to cash in on coffee as a from-home

work opportunity. You could play old movies in your shop or have a collection of books (often offered for sale) for people to read and browse through while drinking coffee. You could sell taped music of a special period—the big bands, the ballads of the 50s, the music of the 60s and 70s. You could bring in newspapers from major metropolitan cities around the country. Once people know you always have the latest papers from these places, they'll come to your coffee bar to read them.

To make espresso, you must have a commercial espresso machine. Otherwise, you're likely to end up with an inadequate machine that will be too slow. Your customers will grow impatient, go elsewhere, and you'll be out of business.

Almost no one drinks coffee all by itself. Pastries, bagels, and muffins are a necessary part of a coffee bar. These can be purchased wholesale or made from scratch at home. If you make them from scratch, you could become famous not only for your coffee but for your pastries as well.

Another avenue in the coffee business is to create a retail and wholesale distribution and sales operation for coffee beans. One couple began such an operation by going directly to the coffee roasters to purchase beans. They made an initial investment of about $12,000 for coffee and supplies. Then they contacted gourmet coffee shops and offered to supply them with a variety of coffee roasts in whole bean form. They also set up displays in markets in their area. In their first month they grossed about $300. Two years later in the same month of the year they grossed $5000.

If the idea appeals to you, be sure to do your research before launching out. Ask yourself, "Has my area caught on to the gourmet coffee idea, or would I have to educate the public before I could build a clientele?" This might save you from launching a business prematurely.

If you love coffee and people, and have a house in a high traffic area, an espresso shop is a possibility for your from-home business.

Grow Gourmet Vegetables

Start-up cost: $1,000 for seeds, fertilizers, and garden tools. If you need a truck to move the produce, it might cost you $4,000 to $5,000 for a used truck or van.

Break-even: One gardening season—three to five months

Annual income: $10,000 to $12,000 per acre of land planted. (This makes a good part-time or extra income home job.)

We're not talking "garden variety" vegetables. These are exotic specialties like purple potatoes and tiny squashes. Specialty restaurants look for unusual vegetables and herbs to give their cuisine a distinctive and unique look.

If growing strange-looking vegetables appeals to you, start searching gardening books and seed catalogs for the unusual and start planting, selling, and reaping not only veggies, but profits. Price your vegetables at four times what it costs you to grow them.

Low-fat, Low-cal Lunch Delivery

Start-up cost: $500 for coolers, licenses, and advertising flyers

Break-even: One to two months

Annual income: $25,000 to $40,000

If someone would deliver a low-cal, low-fat lunch to my office he would have a regular customer. I'm not talking about the galley wagon that sells hot dogs and ham and egg sandwiches; I'm talking about someone who hands me a menu on Friday to order my lunches for the next week—wholesome soups that may need a couple of minutes in the microwave, low-fat sandwiches on whole grain breads, and fresh fruit or yogurt.

To start this business the only equipment you need is a car to make deliveries and a couple of food chests. You also need a place to prepare the food. One man who started this way a few years ago now delivers 3,000 sandwiches, salads, and other items each day. His simple from-home idea has turned into a full-time business and he must now employ people to help him make and distribute food all over the city.

What if each sandwich went for $3 or $4 each and cost $.50 to make? Pretty good profit!

All of the starter business ideas I've listed use only one or two simple pieces of equipment. If I've piqued your interest and helped you believe that you, too, can work from home, then, as you begin to consider what you might do, you'll think of even more ideas on your own.

CHAPTER FIVE

Craft Ideas to Earn From-Home Dollars

Talk about proliferation! Craft businesses are multiplying faster than rabbits and making lots of money, too. Most full-time craft businesses gross anywhere from $40,000 to $200,000 a year. Making crafts can be a source of supplemental income, a part-time job, or a profitable full-time job.

Handmade is in. Take, for example, hand-painted furniture. With a minimal start-up cost of only $200 to $400 you can buy a number of used furniture pieces and paint supplies. If this is your craft of choice, look for good solid pieces of furniture, strip and paint them, and then, depending on your expertise, tole paint them (requires some expertise) or stencil them (can be learned in a few minutes). Resell as soon as possible, buy more pieces, and repeat the process. You should be able to bring in at least $25,000 a year, even if you are only working part time. You'll make more if you are doing custom work.

Friends of mine underwrote several trips to Europe by finding furniture that needed only minimal work to make it usable. They found the furniture at garage sales, thrift stores, and even tossed out in the garbage. They would put on new knobs, tighten joints, and either paint or refinish the pieces. Then they would have their own garage sale and sell the refurbished pieces at a huge profit.

The markup on decorated, refinished furniture is excellent. For example, a $5 table when decorated could sell for $65, and the person who is buying it is getting a one-of-a-kind treasure at a better price than if he were buying it at a furniture store. You are also recycling durable goods.

Such a craft is easy to learn. Paint stores offer classes, you can pick up dozens of books on the subject, and there are classes through community programs and vo-tech schools.

DISCOVERING THE NEXT IDEA

Let's take a look at some simple yet profitable crafts you can do from your kitchen table. When we finish this chapter, we will have only begun, because the next idea for a craft is out there just waiting to be discovered.

The truly successful makers of crafts are those who travel to craft shows and display and sell their wares. Some craft makers log as many as 40,000 miles a year traveling to shows. Pick shows carefully, and after some experimentation, pick only the best ones to cut down on travel and expense. Decide ahead of time if you want to take orders at shows and sell crafts by mail order.

QUESTIONS TO ASK

Before you plunge in with all your energy and resources, ask yourself some questions:

1. *What do customers want?* There are 6,000 craft fairs in this country each year. And they are jam-packed with craftspeople and customers. Besides craft shows, you can sell crafts at county and state fairs, gift shops, boutiques, swap

meets, and major department stores. With that many outlets, the first question to ask before going into the crafts business full time is, "What might customers be looking for that isn't yet available?" Do not despair, there is something.

2. *How is my craft unique?* It's worth it to establish a craft with your unique "signature." Adding that personalized twist will sell your crafts if you've answered the first question, "Is this something people want?"

3. *Is there a need for the craft?* Sometimes you have to create a need. Think of all the things you'd like to have. How many of them even existed ten years ago? Why didn't you need them then, and why do you think you need them now? Because someone has convinced you of your need. You may have to do the same persuasion for your craft.

4. *How inexpensively can I begin?* The beauty of making crafts is that you usually don't need a huge outlay of money to get started. You can buy $20 worth of fabric and turn it into half a dozen dolls that sell for $20 each. Now you have $180 for supplies and you're launched.

5. *How much time must I devote to my craft?* I have seen more than one money-making venture falter because the idea was so good the maker of the product couldn't keep up with demand. Customers don't respond well to wanting something immediately and not being able to get it. If you start a successful business, you'll have to keep the pipeline flowing to your customers.

6. *Do I have an outlet for my craft?* There are all kinds of ways to sell crafts, from ads in newspapers and magazines to setting up at crafts fairs. Without an outlet, you won't be successful. Plan how you will sell your product before you fill your basement with handcrafted items.

CREATE A SPECIAL LABEL

It's a bit of a nuisance and an expense, but your own personalized hangtag (that little label attached to a product that gives your company's name and the price of the object) is some of the best advertising you can buy. And while you're having a hangtag designed and printed, have matching business cards made up as well.

A well-designed hangtag speaks of quality and the professional image of the crafts person. It gives instant recognition of the product or maker for repeat orders.

Tags vary in size, shape, color, design, the type of paper used, and the information printed on them. They must have your logo, telephone number, address, and the price of the product. You can also add a slogan, handling and care information, labeling of contents, and if the craft has a unique history—such as a historic design—put that information on the label. Prices can be handwritten and attached to the card with stickers that peel off easily for customers who are giving the items as gifts.

If you are short on ideas for designing a hangtag, visit some craft fairs and see what others do. Decide which hangtags attract you and why. Then design your own.

On a vacation in New England, I purchased several Christmas tree ornaments with a distinctive hangtag. On one side of the recycled paper tag was an oval circle with a hand in the middle. The hand was holding a heart, and the words around the oval read, "Hand-crafted with care." The back of the tag read, "Crafted in the tradition of an earlier time, when all production was completed by hand. The subtle difference in color, size, texture, and character express the unique identity of each piece."

There are federal and state laws requiring labeling on certain crafts. To find out if your product requires a special label, write or call the Federal Trade Commission or the U.S. Consumer Product Safety Commission at:

Federal Labeling Laws
Bureau of Consumer Protection
Federal Trade Commission
6th St. and Pennsylvania Ave. N.W.
Washington, D.C. 20580
Telephone: (202) 326-2222

Compliance Office
U.S. Consumer Products
Safety Commission
4330 East West Highway
Bethesda, MD 20814
Telephone: (301) 504-0400, ext. 1378

Now for information about some specific businesses.

Chair Caning

Start-up cost: $100-$1,000 for equipment, supplies, advertising
Break-even: Two to six months
Annual income: $12,500 to $24,000

This is a specialty craft in great demand by restorers of antique furniture and makers of reproduction furniture. A chair that has broken caning is worthless, but when restored, the chair immediately becomes valuable again.

Work for a while with someone who knows caning and learn the craft. Then practice on some flea market pieces. Soon you'll be ready to try work for your customers.

You can charge about $50 for a chair that has 100 holes. That's a small chair seat. You can charge four times that price for full cane-backed and cane-seated chairs.

Set up a work area at an antique show or shop and have some of your finished pieces on display. Particularly effective would be a before and after chair.

To add to your income:

- Teach caning at local colleges and parks and recreation departments.
- Collect furniture that needs caning. Repair it and sell it.
- Collect baskets, wicker furniture and repair and sell them.
- Write articles or a book on the subject.

Gift Baskets
   Start-up cost: $2,000 to $10,000 for supplies, a work room, business cards, advertising
   Break-even: Six months to one year
   Annual income: $30,000 to $50,000

I've mentioned gift baskets throughout the previous chapters of this book, but now let's truly focus on them and think of ways to make a gift-basket business successful. Successful could mean from $60,000 to $300,000 a year, although the $30,000 to $50,000 listed above is more realistic. To produce more than that you would have to hire staff. Of course, when the business grows, you will want to add staff and find larger quarters for storage of the components that make up the baskets.

It's always important to know what others in your area are charging for gift baskets before setting prices. Gift baskets usually cost from $25 to $85, depending on their contents. The cost of the basket and its contents should be 25 percent of what you charge. One order of 100 baskets can produce income of $3,000 to $4,000.

Once you have your business license, you'll be allowed to

visit wholesale houses and buy baskets and other craft items at wholesale prices. Buying low and selling high is essential to making a profit.

You might also keep an eye on local thrift shops. I have bought many handsome baskets for less than a dollar each at thrift shops. Wicker can be scrubbed, painted, or covered with fabric for a whole new look and it doesn't matter where the baskets come from. It's what fills the baskets that is important.

Come up with a look uniquely yours. For instance, you could line baskets with red and white checked fabric, fill them with straw, tie a big gold bow on them, or they could always be delivered with a bunch of balloons tied to the handle. This is the fun part of creating crafts—making the look your own.

In the beginning, try different kinds of baskets and see what works best for you. Then produce and reproduce the baskets that work, and sell them like crazy.

Think of products that can only be found in your region. If I were in the gift basket business in the northwest, I'd start with a good-sized basket to hold the many wonderful products available, and I'd line it with something very green, because almost everything in the northwest is green.

I'd start with a small tin of smoked salmon. I'd add a couple of small samplers of Starbucks coffee (Starbucks got its start in Seattle). I'd put in two or three of the shiniest Washington Delicious apples I could find. Then I'd tuck in a couple of jars of blackberry and raspberry jam and a small package of Fishers scone mix—a northwestern product. A small box of Aplets or Cotlets candy (made in Cashmere, Washington) and some Almond Roca (made in Tacoma, Washington) would complete the basket—unless you wanted to throw in a rain gauge for the fun of it.

I'd tie up the whole thing with a big plaid bow appropriate to the season—red and green for Christmas, fall colors for Thanksgiving, or pastels for Easter.

Then I'd contact firms that have clients in other parts of the country and get them to tell me how many baskets they need for their A-1 customers.

What products are unique to your area? Here in Colorado, it might be a strand of red-hot chili peppers, salsa, or chili seasoning. In Maine it might be a small handcrafted item like a wooden butter spreader, or it might be a tin of real maple syrup. From the deep South, pralines or cornbread "fixin's."

If the gift basket is for the birth of a new baby, fill it with practical items—swabs, baby shampoo, washcloths and towels, a baby spoon, a pacifier, a toy. Tie it up with a helium-filled balloon printed with congratulatory words about the baby's arrival.

If the basket is for a wedding, fill it with kitchen tools, a cookbook for two, specialty pastas and condiments, some spices, a pot of herbs, and lay it all on a couple of place mats with some matching napkins tucked in.

A basket for an elderly person's birthday could include hard candies, specialty cookies, a little memory or verse book, framed pictures of family members provided by the giver of the basket, a tiny imported pill box, and a pretty handkerchief for the ladies or some big red bandannas for the men.

If you lack ideas, visit a specialty food store and see what they have to offer in gift baskets and at what price. Talk to others who make baskets and modify their ideas to fit your own purposes.

While you are in the specialty food and gift shops, ask them if you can provide their gift baskets. Get them to buy outright and not take your baskets on consignment. Consignment means you have to wait too long for your money, and if you don't have money, you can't produce more baskets.

Other ways to find customers:

- Call on corporate and organizational buyers and leave sample baskets for the decision makers.
- Go on a local TV show and demonstrate how to put together gift baskets.
- Have gift basket parties, similar to Tupperware parties.
- Exhibit at craft and home shows.
- Build a direct-mail list and mail to it periodically.
- Donate baskets to charities and other nonprofit organizations if they will include your company name in their program and mention it from the podium.
- Network and make personal contacts in organizations, business associations, and church groups. Occasionally provide a gift basket for a door prize.

Jewelry Crafting
Start-up cost: $1,000 to $5,000 for materials and advertising
Break-even: Two to six months
Annual income: $25,000 to $50,000

Jewelry can be made from many different materials: gold, silver, semi-precious and precious stones. It can also be made from bits of wire, clay, ceramic, shells, and much more.

Your costs to get into jewelry crafting will depend on the materials you use. Obviously, gold and silver cost more than clay and shells. You will also be able to sell gold and silver jewelry for a higher price. When pricing jewelry, consider the amount of materials used, the kind of materials, and the time you've invested to make the piece, then price accordingly. To get a better feel for pricing, go to craft shows and observe what others charge for their pieces.

To learn the craft, apprentice with a jewelry maker or take classes at an art center. To display your wares, set up a booth where you actually make jewelry at a craft fair or in a mall.

Sell your pieces through the usual craft outlets, boutiques, and specialty jewelry stores. Take out a small ad in craft magazines and send direct mailings to customers. Good jewelry designers with innovative ideas sell their products easily and quickly.

Bird Houses

Start-up cost: $100 to $2,000 if you need to buy power tools. They aren't necessary but certainly make the job easier.

Break-even: One month to one year

Annual income: $10,000 to $35,000 (part time or combined with other wood-worked projects)

One summer my brother and I made some birdhouses. We assembly-line manufactured them and I saw what a difference the right tools can make. We made bluebird houses with no finish. (Unfinished houses attract the birds.) We made snug wren houses with green metal roofs and learned that it's good to leave an air space just under the roof so the house doesn't get too hot in the summer.

The birdhouse I own that birds like best is an unpainted pine house that I picked up at a craft store for a couple of dollars. I bent a license plate over the top as a roof to keep out the rain. A rusty old license plate adds charm. Put it outside for a season to weather and you end up with a birdhouse that fits into a country decorating motif.

You don't need great carpentry skills to manufacture decorative bird houses. Just go to a craft store, pick up an assortment of unpainted bird houses, and give them a natural finish or paint them in a decorative way, using your own ideas and designs.

On a garden tour last year, I saw a wonderful little birdhouse painted all over with flowers in the manner of an

English cottage. It was mounted on a post in the middle of a flower garden. While birds couldn't care less how a house looks, people are delighted by such a pretty little house.

Suppose you could figure out a way to make a birdhouse that was a miniature of the owner's house. I can't think of anyone who could resist a birdhouse like that. For one-of-a-kind birdhouses and other large birdhouses of a distinctive design, you might charge up to $250. It's true! People will pay that much for something unique and personalized. The amount of time to construct such a birdhouse would depend on your expertise as a carpenter. Probably in the beginning you would have to proceed slowly, but after a while you would have some basic template designs and could construct them more quickly.

If you can purchase birdhouses for less than $10 and decorate them for $1-$2, you should be able to sell them for about $45-$50 dollars.

Quilts
Start-up cost: $100 to $500
Break-even: Upon the sale of your first quilt
Annual income: $30,000 to $50,000

Years ago it was tough to give away a patchwork quilt. Many lay moldering in the bottom of family storage chests. Others had been pieced but not quilted.

Then, kaboom! Everyone started searching for old quilts, making their own, and buying them. Quilts made by the Amish people of Pennsylvania sell for $900 to $1,500 and are worth every penny because they are works of art. Tiny stitches, unusual designs and colors, and a bit of history are all worked into a quilt by these industrious folk. It's possible to sell quilts at $240 to $345 each for a queen-size bed.

Quilts are now recognized as works of art that increase in value every year. You can charge more for a quilt if there are tiny pieces and lots of curves, because they take a lot more work to produce.

Sell quilts through craft shows, interior design studios, and at mall shows.

Toys

Start-up cost: $400 to $1,000 if you already have the necessary tools, more if you don't
Break-even: Two to three months
Annual income: $10,000 part time to $50,000 full time

Recently I had dinner with friends. One of the guests was a new grandfather. He came to dinner late because he had gone shopping for his baby grandson. He had seen a little tool carrier filled with cloth tools. Since this man is an architect, the toy greatly appealed to him.

I remember several years ago seeing a collection of cloth dolls. Two women were sitting in a little doll shop chatting away and sewing details on the dolls' faces—or maybe they were embroidering belly buttons, because all these dolls had them. The dolls were completely charming and I had a strong urge to pick them up and squeeze them. Sales and orders were brisk for these two women.

Another woman, Akira Blount of Bybee, Tennessee, makes and sells collector dolls for $500 and up. Her company grosses $150,000 a year. She taught herself to make dolls and just kept making them until she found a niche in the market and had gained expertise. Part of her success came when she joined two major craft guilds.[1] (Information about craft guilds at the end of this chapter.)

Handmade wooden toys also have great appeal. They continue to be popular with children and tend to become collectors' items. Among the toys I have retained from my son's growing-up years is a small wooden train. I set it up each

Christmas and will probably never part with it.

After many years, Barbie dolls and all the members of her entourage are still popular. If you can stand to sew tiny garments, you can still sell them. Also, Barbie can use bed linens, tiny beach towels, hats, and many other doll accessories.

After a hundred years, teddy bears are still popular. They can be dressed in hundreds of ways and can be made of everything from flannel, calico, and terry cloth to fake fur, real fur, and leather. You can dress them in tutus, mountain climbing gear, black ties and tails, or peasant dresses. Once again, you're only limited by imagination. Watch catalogs, toy shops, and specialty shops for ideas.

Toys can be crocheted, knitted, sewn, stuffed, carved, and constructed. All you need to produce a highly saleable toy is to find a tiny twist that makes the toy your own design.

If toy-making appeals to you, remember that safety is a key factor. There must be no small parts children can pull off and put into their mouths or stuff up their noses. Find out what safety regulations are in effect for your state and county and what federal regulations might apply. (Write to the Federal Safety Commission at Bureau of Consumer Protection, Federal Trade Commission, 6th St. and Pennsylvania Ave. N.W., Washington, D.C. 20580).

To extend your income from toy making, sell patterns for the toys and ready-to-be-assembled kits, as well as the finished products.

I have only scratched the surface of ideas for toy making. Check out books from the library and go to craft fairs and toy shops to see what others are making. Perhaps half the fun of toy making comes from getting to stay a child yourself as you dream up and make the toys. The other half might be the joy you see when a child embraces a toy you have made.

Christmas (Holiday) Decorative Items
Start-up cost: $500-$1,000
Break-even: One to two months
Annual income: $5,000 to $10,000 (seasonal)

This is not necessarily a seasonal job. Christmas crafts are now available all year.

Since there are whole books on the subject of Christmas crafts and every year popular magazines offer dozens more new ideas, this book will only offer a sampling of craft ideas. Hopefully, those ideas will spark new ideas and help you realize that you, too, can reap financial reward from your craft ideas.

Ornaments
Christmas tree ornaments are sold year round. When I travel, I'm always looking for an unusual ornament to bring home as a reminder of the trip or to give away.

Regional ornaments—those that have something to do with your region of the country should sell well all year. Let's brainstorm some regional ornament ideas.

- If you live in the Seattle area or near New York City, why not make a ferry boat ornament?
- What about a streetcar for San Francisco or New Orleans?
- If you live in a wooded area, dip pine cones in silver paint, spray with glue, and roll in glitter that looks like crystal flakes.
- Find small unpainted wooden ducks, loons, and other waterfowl and handpaint them to look like a regional waterfowl.
- If your area is famous for the fruit it grows, create replicas, perhaps on wood or clay, as Christmas tree ornaments—a shiny red apple, a luscious peach, a cluster of strawberries, or an orange. Do something to make it different. The

orange could have a cluster of silk orange blossoms attached; the apple could have a bite taken out of it.

I've already mentioned an ornament I bought in New England that had a distinctive hangtag. That ornament looks like a wooden box with wire handles. On the side is painted the word "cranberries." The box is filled with miniature imitation fruit and retailed for about $6. This is an ornament with a regional appeal, and while I don't live in the area, I bought it as a reminder of my trip.

Wreaths

Wreaths are an integral part of Christmas and there are thousands of ideas for their design. Here in the Southwest we use a lot of red peppers for wreaths. In the Northwest it's cedar, balsam, and fir—very traditional. In the Northeast it's also evergreens—lots of balsam. An Italian community might like a wreath made from pasta products or one that looks like a traditional Della Robbia.

Straw wreaths can be decorated with toys and red-and-white checked or plaid bows; grapevine wreaths can be decorated with shiny balls. You can even pin brightly-colored pieces of candy to wreaths—the possibilities are endless.

Wreaths that need to be shipped will require special handling, so talk with a box manufacturer about suitable boxes. I have received fragile dried wreaths that were wired to the boxes by inserting a wire from the outside of the bottom of the box in two or three places and twisting it around the wreath on the inside to hold it in place. Then tissue paper was packed into the corners of the box and center of the wreath before the top was replaced. A packer or shipper should be able to help you figure out how to ship your wreaths and may even do it for you for a fee.

Table Linens

Many people like special tablecloths and napkins for the holidays. You can find beautiful fabrics in all kinds of patterns and designs. All you have to do is hem them.

You might consider taking custom orders for tablecloths so the size would exactly fit the customer's table. Promise a date to have the cloth ready and then deliver on time.

Clothing

Hand-crafted clothing is sold in boutiques and specialty shops all across the country.

One of my favorite places on earth is Pike Place Market in Seattle. In this old farmers' market, fresh food, fish, flowers, and handcrafts vie for the shoppers' attention. There are also many clothing stalls with handpainted T-shirts for babies, appliquéed ethnic style clothes, leather coats, skirts, handbags, and vests.

If you have a good sewing machine, a flair for design, and this idea appeals to you, think about a specialty item that would appeal to a broad spectrum of people.

What about making hand-smocked dresses for baby girls? Smocking is fairly easy to learn from books and is taught in sewing classes and parks and recreations programs. Watch the paper for classes. How about baby outdoor wraps and little sailor suits or fluffy dresses with appliqués?

You can proceed right up through the ranks of age in creating handmade clothes. Once again, find something unique.

- For teenage girls, learn how to make those big, floppy hats of velvet and denim and all kinds of wonderful fabrics.
- For teen guys, make vests in all kinds of fabrics and patterns or vests showing their favorite sport or hobby.
- For the elderly, design and make brightly colored, soft textured, easy-to-put-on clothing with snaps, Velcro closings,

and buttons in the front. Make the garments big and roomy enough to pull over their heads but also snug and warm. (I encourage you to investigate this growing field.)

Tin-Crafting

Start-up cost: $500 for hammers, tin cutters, awls, nails, files, and soldering tools
Break-even: One to two months
Annual income: $35,000 to $60,000

A few years ago I moved into a house I had built. I knew exactly what style of furnishings I wanted—country in the informal areas and a style that was a bit English in the dining room and living room.

Just before the move, I went to a huge craft show where one of the merchants was a tinsmith. There, hanging in his display, was the perfect light fixture for my kitchen eating area. It was a eight-armed tin chandelier with holders for real candles. But there was also a down light to illuminate the eating area. It was exactly what I wanted and I asked him to make one for me.

I also needed two hanging lights over the stove area. This presented a problem because they needed to match the tin chandelier. I asked the tinsmith if he thought he could make some hanging lights from punched tin if I provided a picture. He was sure he could and he did.

When it came time to pay him, he asked for very little because I had challenged him and given him a new design. Along the way I also showed him a number of other antique chandelier designs, which he hoped to duplicate.

Tinsmithing is a craft as old as this country. In colonial times, smiths punched tin for lanterns and constructed big tin chandeliers for public buildings. Candles were placed in tin sconces that sometimes were polished to reflect the light. Tin-crafting is still in demand because home decorators love the colonial country style. A tinsmith can make not only lighting devices but useful household objects, decorative objects, and even toys.

If tin-crafting appeals to you, you might apprentice yourself to a tinsmith.

Carving and Specialty Wooden Items
Start-up cost: $200 for knife, blanks, and lessons
Break-even: One project
Annual income: $30,000 to $36,000

Once again, the interest in handmade country items feeds the demand for wood carving. There are many inexpensive carvings on the market that have been made in China and other Asian countries. But that's not what we are talking about here. Go to a specialty store that sells true handcrafted items and just look at the prices charged for hand-carving. Carved birds of all kinds demand the highest prices. Five hundred dollars would be a reasonable price for a large hand-carved duck.

While it might be difficult to make a living by carving, it could certainly provide an excellent supplemental income, and you could also feed a creative part of your soul.

Other hand-carved items that continue to have high appeal are nativity scenes and Noah's Ark sets complete with pairs of animals.

Although we often think of wood carvers as being men, women can enjoy this craft as well. You could start simply by making wooden kitchen utensils and handles for kitchen utensils. Take a couple of classes or get someone to show you how to use the necessary power tools.

Bed and Bath Linens
   Start-up cost: $500 for linens and trims
   Break-even: Your first sale
   Annual income: $20,000 to $40,000

Americans seem to have gone crazy over bed linens. While there are hundreds of patterns of sheets, pillowcases, and towels available, there is still room for the creative person to make specialty linens.

Plain 100 percent cotton sheets and pillowcases can be dressed up by adding lace, hand embroidery, purchased appliqués, ribbons, plaid, or calico trim. In the time it takes to sew it on, you've changed a plain-Jane pillowcase into a lovely decorative item.

There are several programs on public television that explain how to make some of these specialty items. You can also order videos from these programs or obtain videos from fabric stores and learn how to make decorative linens.

Sell your linens through the usual craft outlets and through interior design shops. Contact interior designers about creating one-of-a-kind looks for their customers.

Knitting, Crocheting, and Other Needlework
   Start-up cost: $200 for needles, yarns, threads, accessories
   Break-even: After two or more projects
   Annual income: $10,000 (part time)

There is a resurgence of love for needlework crafts. One of the big craft items at the Pike Place Market is heavy, hand-knitted sweaters—outdoor sweaters. Only a short time ago we threw out or hid in trunks the crocheted doilies and antimacassars our grandmothers made so lovingly and gave to us. We simply didn't know what to do with them because they were out of fashion. Now they're back in but being used for everything from dresses for angels to ornaments for handbags.

Perhaps you could make your specialty white-on-white linens. That means high quality white linens, white embroidery, and white crocheted or knitted trim. White-on-white linens are very popular. You can add a distinctive touch by adding just a bit of blue, pink, rose, or orchid-colored ribbon.

Hand-knitted items are treasured and handed down from generation to generation. Doting grandparents will buy hand-knit garments for their grandbabies, and, since there are more doting grandparents than ever before and more babies than we've had in a long time, this is a growing market.

Sell through local craft shops, mall and craft shows, hospital gift shops, and clothing stores that cater to mothers and babies. Run a small classified ad in your local newspaper or in national magazines.

Weaving

Start-up cost: $300 to $1,000 for loom and supplies
Break-even: One to three months
Annual income: $10,000 to $15,000

Weaving is a wonderful craft requiring a big workroom and some heavy-duty equipment, but the results of handcrafted weaving are wonderful. Those who weave say it is one of the most therapeutic of all crafts. There's something comforting about the monotony of the shuttle going back and forth.

Handwoven crafts include everything from woolen shawls, capes, and caps to table linens designed from colonial patterns. Weavers are reproducing those wonderful old woolen coverlets early settlers placed on their beds. The intricate patterns are still a challenge to weavers today.

You can start small by weaving belts on a small simple loom. A slightly larger loom enables you to make placemats and napkins. Some looms—the smaller ones—come with instructions that are easy to follow. Learn how to use the larger looms by taking classes at a local weaving shop. Most cities of any size have weaving shops.

Weaving is one of the oldest, most practical crafts, and the end result of your labors at a loom should sell at top dollar through specialty shops, antique stores, designer dress shops, boutiques, and craft shows. You might even be able sell them through historical museums such as Plymouth Plantation, Williamsburg, and Old Sturbridge Village. A simple advertisement in several women's magazines could bring excellent direct-mail possibilities.

Candles

Start-up cost: $500 to $4,000 for supplies, a workroom, and office
Break-even: Two months to one year
Annual income: $15,000 to $45,000

Since ancient times people have used candles as a source of light. Today candles are also used for decorative purposes and to create atmosphere.

I had a friend whose philosophy of home entertainment included the use of a lot of candles. If she had been very busy at work on a day she planned to entertain, she would get some food from a deli, pick up the newspapers and other things lying about the house, turn down the lights, and light candles.

She had a reputation for being a gracious hostess, but the truth was she didn't fuss with a lot of dusting, sweeping, and other typical preparations. Part of her success was the cozy atmosphere created by candles.

It seems as if the interest in decorative candles has (please forgive the pun) waxed and waned. But there is always a demand for candles.

You could make handcarved candles, layered candles, a set of candles of various sizes, shapes, and shades of the same color. Add candle holders of all kinds to your stock and teach candle-making classes at local community colleges and parks and recreation departments. If you can write, sell articles about candle-making.

You could sell your candles at a weekend craft show or at home parties. You could advertise your candles at bridal shops, home and garden shows, or as part of an interior designer's display.

OTHER WAYS TO MAKE MONEY FROM CRAFTS

Another way to make money from crafts is to open a craft consignment store and take a percentage of the earnings from the crafts you sell. This can be a from-home business if you establish the store in your garage or a spare room. Good advertising is essential so that people can find your shop.

Get your crafters to help you by providing them with flyers

Ways to Market Your Crafts

Craft shows—Need to enter 20 to 25 a year to make it pay. Requires travel, booth fees, and transport of your craft items to the show.

Wholesaling—Sell to a retailer who adds a markup and resells your craft.

Co-op Sales—You and other crafters lease a store and take turns staffing it.

Consignment—The store takes a percentage of what you earn.

Direct Sales—You build your own customer base through a mailing list and direct sales to customer.

to hand out that say, "See my craft items at _____."
Include a map, hours of operation, your logo, and any other
information that would create interest.

This chapter is only a small sampling of the things you
might do to make and sell handcrafts. It is only meant to be an
idea starter. By investigating, observing, reading, and playing
with ideas, you should be able to develop a market that suits
your talents and interests and maximizes your creativity as well
as reap a healthy financial reward.

RESOURCES

Organizations
American Craft Council
(212) 274-0630
Has shows, offers group insurance, and publishes *American
Craft* magazine. Ask them about guilds.

Trade Journals:
Sunshine Artist
422 W. Fairbanks Ave. Suite 300
Winter Park, FL 32789
1-800-597-2573

CHAPTER SIX

Using Your Computer for Your From-Home Business

S omeone has said that when computers replace people on a job (and they do every day) it's good to be the person running the computer. Soon the bulk of information will be passed electronically, and those who know how to access it will be the ones who move forward quickly and with confidence.

I once listened to an interview with James Michener, who is at the writing of this book eighty-eight years old. He had just finished another massive novel called *Recessional*. The interviewer asked him about how he writes his novels. He does it on an old (1940s) typewriter. She then asked him if he had any interest in using a computer for word processing. His reply was, "I'm not stupid. As soon as I have my rough draft my secretary puts it on the word processor and we do all our editing there. I wouldn't be without it."[1] If James Michener at eighty-eight can find a way to use a word processor, so can we.

An amazing variety of work can be accomplished with a home computer and its accessories (modem, fax modem, etc.) Even as I write these words, someone is thinking up a new idea for using the home computer for work, or is inventing a new program for making whatever you conceive easier to do. There are thousands of computer applications yet to be discovered and you just might be the one to do it.

Word Processing

Start-up cost: $5,000 to $10,000, depending on how much equipment you will need to add and the kind of equipment you choose.

Break-even: Six months to one year

Annual income: $22,500 to $45,000

Word processing is the granddaddy of computer uses. Many people have gone into the field and the competition is fierce. Getting the price you need may be more difficult than in some other computer-based operations. The free-lance word processing people I have used charge about $2 per page. That price includes keyboarding and proofreading their own work. If they are keyboarding information off a tape, the price is higher—about $2.50 to $3 per page. Industry rates are $2 to $7.50 per page, $15 to $30 an hour, or $1 per 1,000 characters.

Find a niche and fill it. Specialize in something such as law transcription, scriptwriting, or medical transcription. Find something unique to offer your customers, such as after hours word processing or specialty word processing, such as court transcribing or inputting theses for graduate students.

Equipment and software needs are simple. Computers range from $1,500 to $4,000. Find a software package you are comfortable using and that provides some options for formatting and page design. A software package will cost $250 to $500. Purchase a high quality printer—an ink jet or laser printer. This is probably the most important piece of equipment you will buy. It should offer a variety of fonts and options. Expect to pay $1,600 to $2,500 for a quality printer.

To find customers, advertise on bulletin boards at colleges, libraries, and supermarkets. Contact law firms, hospitals, and banks. Advertise in the yellow pages. Follow up on help-wanted classified ads for word processing to see what is needed.

Contact other word processing services and tell them you will take their overflow work.

Word processing is an excellent occupation for supplementing income, and as part-time or full-time work from home.

Desktop Publishing
Start-up cost: $2,000 to $6,000
Break-even: Six months to one year
Annual income: $25,000 to $40,000

Desktop publishing grew out of improvements in word-processing and graphics software. It is now possible to format and design pages in many ways and with many graphics features. It is possible to format books, newsletters, children's books, and much more. Many desktop publishers design brochures, pamphlets, and other information pieces for companies. They may also design and produce direct-mail pieces—everything from catalogs to return devices such as postage-paid mail-in cards.

The work is interesting and creative and the field is growing. However, it is also increasingly competitive. To remain current with the advances in technology, you need to upgrade your software frequently. If you have a flair for design, or at least can copy another person's design, you have a head start on desktop publishing. The problem with many from-home desktop operations is that the computer operator doesn't understand design, and the piece comes out jumbled and confusing to read. The reader gives up and a customer is lost.

Another problem with desktop publishing is the quality of printing. Printing is really a series of dots laid down on paper. Good printing uses many dots and the quality of printing drops as the dots per inch (DPI) drop. For that reason, many people who do desktop publishing finish the project by printing it on a linotronic printer that gives a DPI of 1,200 to

3,000 as opposed to a computer printer with a DPI of 300 to 1,200. A low DPI gives a ragged edge on large type that is visible to the naked eye.

My company's proofing sheets are produced on a laser printer. They look wonderful, but they are not good enough for the printing process. When we have a clean copy—no more corrections—the typesetters run out the job on a linotronic printer on photographic paper. The linotronic reproduction is very high quality and is ready for printing. It could be that to produce high-quality printing you will need to pay someone to run your copy on a linotronic printer. More and more, presses would just as soon have a computer disk with the book and all the fonts and graphics design inserted.

Advertise a desk-top publishing business by informing printers and others in the typesetting and desktop publishing field that you are in business, and by producing a sales flyer and mailing it to publishers, newspapers, and any company that produces any kind of printed material. Follow up with a phone call and an in-person interview if you can get it. Also advertise in the yellow pages.

Computer Consulting

Start-up cost: $500 (if you have existing clients) to $6,000 to establish a new client base—travel, advertising, long distance telephone

Break-even: Immediate to one year

Annual income: $50,000 to $250,000

If you have expertise in computer systems and understand what the right computer system can do for a company, computer consulting could be your cup of tea. With the burgeoning growth in computer usage and applications, and because those computers are being operated by people who have little training, consultants are in high demand and will continue to be in demand. Computer consulting consists of selecting the appropriate computer system, networks, and software, and showing the client how to integrate the computer into day-to-day management. The consultant's purpose is to show businesses how a computer system can make them more productive.

If you can find a specialty field for your consulting business, you might do even better. Perhaps your specialty is medical needs or banking or small businesses.

Most successful consultants start small—a job or two in a field they know well—then their business begins to grow by word-of-mouth referrals. The beauty of this business is the low overhead. You don't need to manufacture anything, store anything, or have a huge or fancy office. A desk in the corner of a bedroom, a phone, and a personal computer are all you need.

Computer consultants charge from $25 to $135 per hour. Rates are higher in metropolitan areas and for larger corporations. Rates will vary depending on the kind of company for which you are consulting and the complexity of the problem to be solved.

To enter this field you must know what you are doing. You probably already know quite a bit and that is why you are reading this chapter. If you encounter a problem beyond your expertise, you can buy help. Hire a free-lancer to assist you in the areas where you are weak. If you know the problem is beyond your expertise before you begin, recommend another free-lancer to your client. You may not make any money by recommending someone else, but keep in touch with the client and perhaps, later on, there will be work for you, too.

As in most fields, if you can do it, it's possible you can also write about it, or perhaps teach it. Consider writing for computer magazines and/or teaching at a local high school, an adult education program, or a community or recreational program.

There are a number of fine books on the subject. (See resource guide.) If this is a field that interests you, read, network with other consultants, start small, and let your business grow.

Bookkeeping
Start-up cost: $1,000 to $6,000
Break-even: One to six months
Annual income: $18,000 to $60,000

All businesses need to keep an accurate set of books. Every year more and more small businesses start up and many of the owners have neither the expertise to do their own bookkeeping nor the funds to hire a full-time bookkeeper. They are dependent on free-lance bookkeepers.

If you are good with numbers and you know how to use a spreadsheet, this could be the from-home business for you. You will need a computer; a laptop computer can do anything a full-sized computer can do and it would allow you to take all your documentation to a client's office if necessary.

Your services will include such things as keeping the accounts payable and receivable, reconciling bank statements, doing payroll and invoicing, and preparing financial reports to the point where they can be turned over to a tax preparer.

Bookkeepers can usually charge from $15 to $50 per hour.

Marketing your business could include word-of-mouth referrals, contacting small businesses and interviewing with them, a classified ad in the business section of a newspaper, and making speeches or giving seminars about financial matters.

Tax Preparation

Start-up cost: $1,000 to $4,000
Break-even: One to six months
Annual income: $20,000 to $30,000

I remember the agony of trying to do my own taxes—handling forms, keeping up with tax law changes, getting confused and frustrated. My life has been a lot simpler since I've hired a tax preparer.

I take my tax information to his office, he turns on the computer and pulls up my file. I feed him the year's current information, which he inputs directly to the computer. Within an hour and a half, my taxes are finished. He tells me if there are any red flags for the IRS and he gives me a rough estimate of my tax—whether I owe or will receive a refund. The secret to timely, efficient tax preparation is a software system designed for that purpose and expertise in using it.

I'm not the only person who dislikes tax preparation or is tax-preparation disabled. While the work is seasonal, involving four or five months each year, and labor intensive during that time, it is very profitable and may be all the from-home work you need for a year.

If you have the credentials and training, this might be your kind of job.

Information Brokering

Start-up cost: $5,000 to $10,000
Break-even: Six months to one year
Annual income: $25,000 to $75,000

Welcome to the world of information. We're drowning in it, and there's a place for someone to consolidate information into a readily accessible form. Information brokering and research has become a huge industry, estimated at $13 billion per year and growing every year.

An information broker researches information in a special field using on-line computer services. He or she may be doing a legal search for government regulations on a specific project, researching biographical information for a movie production company, or gathering any other information a client would require.

To succeed as an information broker, you must have a love for information and a desire to gather every last piece of information on a particular subject.

Equipment for information brokering can be expensive. You need a computer with a large capacity for information storage, such as a 486 with at least 200 MB hard drive, a fax/modem and CD-ROM drive, software for accounting/billing, database management, word processing, and a good printer to prepare reports for your clients. The total expense for equipment could be about $5,000. But you can charge from $100 to $150 per hour for one-time brokering and $50 per hour for ongoing research. A good broker should be able to net about $75,000 a year.

You will need to be trained in research and have expertise in operating a computer and accessing on-line information. If you are not qualified but have a high interest in this field, you could get the training you need by taking computer classes. You might work for a while for a research firm to learn the principles of research.

Clients can be found in the same ways you find them for other types of work—through advertising in trade journals, the yellow pages, word-of-mouth, and, most importantly, through direct contact with large firms that need research. Your best customers will be those who need research but have neither the staff nor the time to do it. For more information write to: Information Industry Association, 555 New Jersey Ave. NW, Suite 800, Washington, DC 20001.

Electronic Clipping Service
  Start-up cost: $5,000 to $8,000
  Break-even: Six months to one year
  Annual income: $25,000 to $45,000

Close to information brokering is an electronic clipping service. At one time companies hired people to read newspapers,
magazines, and books, cut out relevant articles, and file them.
Today we've put the scissors away and are able to access huge
amounts of information from our personal computers.

Using key words and phrases, a clipper can locate relevant
information and print it out either in its complete form or in
abstract form.

Most clipping services charge a flat rate that takes into consideration the cost of on-line services. The rate must also take
into consideration the number of pieces of information the
client receives.

If you enjoy reading, searching for information, and investigation—and have the computer equipment—you might enjoy
a from-home business in electronic clipping. To become successful you must also have expertise in computerized database
searching.

Computer Tutoring
  Start-up cost: $1,500 to $2,500
  Break-even: Two to six months
  Annual income: $50,000 to $125,000

A large organization can have its own computer training
department, but a small company is at the mercy of hardware
and software support systems that can be almost impossible to
access because everyone else is trying to access them as well. At
the cost of $75 to $125 per hour, a computer tutor could be

called in to help employees get a small business up and running.

To be a computer tutor you need to know how to operate a personal computer and be an expert in at least one software application. Some software companies have training and certification programs to teach their software. Call the software company of your choice and ask how to become certified.

Get the software company that trains you to give you referrals. Ask satisfied customers to give you recommendations. Send flyers to businesses in your community and follow up with phone calls. Advertise in computer publications. Send a quarterly newsletter that highlights upgrades in software and tips for making a computer operation work. Keep your company's name before your clientele, so that when they have a need, they call you and not another firm.

Computer Programming
Start-up cost: $2,500 to $6,000
Break-even: Two to three months
Annual income: $40,000

As one of the fastest growing industries in the country, computer programming is a potentially good from-home business. A programmer can set up the schedule and amount of work he wishes to do. It is important, however, to remember that when a programmer is in the middle of a project, he may have to work long hours and stay with it until complex problems get solved.

The ideal training for a computer programmer is two to five years of programming background and a familiarity with several computer languages and platforms. Programmers' fees can range up to $100 an hour for highly experienced programmers. You'll need the following equipment:

- a computer
- a network system file server set for at least two computers
- a printer
- communications
- a compiler
- miscellaneous software
- a desk
- an ergonomically correct chair

The best way to get business is to make your former employer a client. You could also join business groups and hand out business cards or flyers, teach a class on programming for business people, or contact computer stores about what you do and post your flyer on their community bulletin board. Look in the classified ads for those companies seeking help in the area of your expertise. You may be able to convince them that what they need can be done on a free-lance basis rather than hiring someone to do it in-house.

Technical Writing
   Start-up cost: $1,000 to $2,500
   Break-even: One to two months
   Annual income: $30,000 to $67,000

Every day products are being released that involve new technology. There is a growing need for people who can write news releases, brochures, pamphlets, articles for trade publications, teaching materials, and instruction manuals—especially manuals people can understand.

You're qualified to do technical writing if you have a working knowledge of the field for which you are writing and if you have good writing and editing skills. You must be able to translate technical information into clear, easy-to-understand terms for nontechnical readers.

Manuals are a good from-home project and can bring from $5,000 to $10,000 each. A skilled technical writer should be able to make from $300 to $800 a day. The average rate charged is $35 to $55 per hour.

The best way to get business is to respond to classified ads for writers and convince the business owners and managers that you can do a better job free-lancing than you or anyone else could by being hired to work in-house. You will also need to place ads in business publications, make direct contact with the companies you want to work for, and network with trade associations and computer user groups.

Telephone Answering Service
Start-up cost: $1,500 to $3,000
Break-even: Two to six months
Annual income: $20,000 to $30,000

Even though we now have voice mail, answering machines, and E-mail, there are still companies that would rather have their phones answered by a live person. Businesses of a highly personal nature, such as medical facilities, doctors' offices, and lawyers' offices are among those who want a live body answering the phone rather than a voice-mail recording. Enter the specialized answering service.

There are lots of telephone answering companies, but few of them offer a personalized service where the answering person functions as an administrative assistant. Such a service would be valuable to small business operators such as plumbers, gardeners, tree removal people, and repairmen who have no office staff and are often out in the field working.

The phone company can now set up your phone with different rings for different incoming calls. It's advertised as a certain ring for your teenage daughter and another for your son; but the same system will work for Ajax Plumbing, Mary's

House Cleaning Service, and other businesses who may use your service. Therefore, when you answer their distinctive ring, you can answer with the name of the company being called. You may need to have several phone lines to accommodate your business.

Use your computer to take messages. If your client has a fax machine, you can send the faxed message directly to his office so he doesn't even need to call in for messages. As an administrative assistant telephone answerer, you can decide which calls demand high priority and which can wait. If your client informs you of his private telephone numbers and keeps you informed about his location, you can forward high-priority calls.

The beauty of this from-home business is that you probably already have the equipment you need: a telephone, a personal computer, a caring attitude. Customers will pay from $100 to $200 per month for your services. Check with other answering services in your area for rates.

Reunion, Party, and Wedding Planner
Start-up cost: $1,500 for computer and basic equipment. If you add props and warehouse space, it can go to $60,000.
Break-even: One month to one year
Annual income: $100,000 to $500,000

If you like parties, enjoy people, and know how to plan events, you can become a reunion organizer, a party planner, or a wedding and wedding-reception planner. While people love these events, many don't know how to plan them. Even if they do, they don't want to spend the necessary time making them happen.

To plan each of these events, you will need a computer and project management software to track schedules, keep phone numbers, contacts, prices, and lots of other details. You will also be able to produce invitations, brochures, announcements, and other printed materials for the events.

A reunion planner takes charge of every aspect of the event from guest lists to after-dinner mints. Much of this is very time consuming, as the reunion planner tries to locate class members, mail invitations, take reservations, and handle a host of other details.

A party planner plans events for large corporations, such as a mystery weekend for the employees of the ABZ corporation. The event could be held at an estate with a gothic-styled mansion. As each employee arrives, he or she is given a Sherlock Holmes deerstalker hat, a magnifying glass, and a set of clues. The guest speaker for the weekend could be a well-known mystery writer.

Other possibilities include a kidnapping party where employees of a corporation are kidnapped and taken to an unknown destination for an event. Or how about a Chinese New Year party, costume party, or luau? The party planner has unlimited opportunity for creativity.

A wedding planner works with the bride to plan the ceremony, costuming, flowers, candles, and other church decorations. The planner also plans the reception (which may have a theme), live music, a dinner, a cake, and special touches the planner can provide, such as balloons, arches with roses, beautiful punch bowls, silver service, uniformed servers or volunteer friends. A good wedding planner is much in demand.

Party planners either plan the entire event or parts of it. They can either do all the elements themselves or buy the cakes and the helium-filled balloons, and lease the props from a rental agency or costume store. In the beginning, this is the way a party planner should proceed, but after a while it may be easier to own your own props. One friend of mine, who does weddings, has all her own decorative table skirts, punch bowls, and silver service.

Planners of large-scale events, who plan several a year, should do well financially. Pay is usually based on a percentage of the registration (10 to 15 percent) in the case of a reunion, and a flat fee for a wedding (usually also 10 to 15 percent of the wedding budget). Check with others in your area to see what they are charging.

If event planning appeals to you, contact colleges and high schools, military units, and large families as clients. For party planning, advertise in business journals, contact corporations, churches, and healthcare organizations. For wedding planning, advertise, post notices in places where bridal gowns are sold, in churches, in floral shops, and in businesses that rent candelabra and other wedding decorations.

You can get training by volunteering to help those who are planning such events. Go to bridal shows and attend seminars and workshops. Work in the catering business. Offer to plan office parties where you now work.

There is a publication for planners: *Special Events*, P.O. Box 8987, Malibu, CA 90265-8987.

Editing
Start-up cost: $1,500 to $2,500
Break-even: One to three months
Annual income: $35,000 to $70,000

There are several levels of editorial work. The highest level is substantive or developmental editing in which an editor assists a writer in the creation and development of a manuscript. Fees for this kind of editing can run from $2,000 to $4,500, although I know it's possible to charge even more, depending on your experience and network.

Line editing is a process in which the editor goes through the manuscript sentence by sentence, tightening and rewording as needed. The editor may also rearrange sentences and paragraphs to make the manuscript as reader-friendly as possible.

Another level of editing is copyediting. This is the person who makes sure all the grammar is correct, the spelling and punctuation are right, and all the stated facts have been checked. This editor excels in detail. Fees for this kind of editing average about $12 to $30 per hour.

The last level of editing is that of proofreading. This is the editor who makes the last pass through the printed material to make sure every error is caught. The fees generally run between $.50 and $.75 a page.

The computer has revolutionized the editing process and your major expense as an editor will be the purchase of a computer and printer. Now, with the flick of a wrist and the punch of a button, an editor can indicate italics, boldface type, choose a different font, or index a manuscript. It's possible to see what a page will look like when it is finished (before it's finished), to apply design with boxes and other graphics, or to set copy in columns.

An editor can use a computerized thesaurus, a spell checker, and a grammatical checker to verify the accuracy of a manuscript. It almost sounds as if the computer does it all for you. That's not quite the case, but it does make accuracy and speed an important part of the process.

An editor needs excellent grammar and language skills, a sense of what works and what doesn't, an ability to straighten out confused thinking on the part of the writer, patience, and an appreciation for the author's style. He also needs to be able to work with people, namely the author, to create the best product possible.

To find work, contact publishing houses to see if they are using free-lance editors. Watch the classified ads in the newspaper for companies that are looking for writers and editors. Approach them about doing the free-lance work. Network with publishing people and groups to learn who's looking for help. If you're good, you'll stay busy.

Free-lance Writing
Start-up cost: $1,500 to $2,000
Break-even: One project or six months
Annual income: $10,000 (part time) to $200,000

Because a computer is fast, stores lots of information, and permits you to make changes without rekeying the text, a free-lancer can write in bits and pieces.

From a home computer you can write articles for all kinds of magazines and for all kinds of fees. You can write books. You can write copy for catalogs and book jackets. You can write copy for ad agencies and direct-mail pieces.

I have a few friends who are making a living by writing. They've been at it for years and have established themselves as writers and have a wide following. They are able to write two or three books a year and bring in advances that allow them to write full time. Advances run from a few thousand dollars to the six-figure range. Of course, the few thousand dollar advances will not allow you to have a full-time career unless you also get out and speak about your subject. After you have a few books in print, there are also some residual royalties from earlier books. A small book I wrote several years ago brings in anywhere from $1,200 to $2,500 a year.

Most successful writers began by writing magazine articles in their spare time, trying out ideas, and acquiring a style of their own. Some worked on church letters or denominational papers. Then they moved on to writing books. Some writers aren't writers at all but are speakers and promoters. They hire someone to do their writing.

Essential to writing are good ideas and good language skills—an ability to communicate what you know. If you have a desire to write but lack skills, get into an adult education program at a local college, take a correspondence course, read analytically to see how others write, read books on writing, go to writers' conferences, and start writing something every day. Polish your best ideas and start submitting them to newspapers and magazines. Above all, be persistent.

Graphic Design
Start-up cost: $5,000 to $15,000
Break-even: Six months to one year
Annual income: $25,000 to $150,000

Computers offer wonderful opportunities in the field of graphic design. Of course, the operator of the computer has to have training and design ability to become successful.

If it is your heart's desire to become a graphic artist, you probably already have an artistic bent. But you probably shouldn't venture into this career unless you have training in basic design principles or are willing to get training through a college or by working in a design or publishing firm.

Graphic designers work on everything from books, magazines, and posters to pamphlets, brochures, newsletters, letterhead, and business cards. They can also design signs, menus for restaurants, T-shirts, forms, programs, advertising pieces, and lots more.

Since most of us are graphics impaired, we are dependent on graphic designers to make us and our businesses look good. Graphic design lends itself nicely to a from-home business. Once the clientele is built, the graphic designer should be able to stay quite busy.

Earnings vary widely, depending on the skill of the designer, the kind of work being done, the level of design—whether four-color or one-color—the amount of time spent working on projects, and many other factors. Graphic designers can charge from $50 to $100 an hour, but first find out what other designers in your area are charging so you don't price yourself out of the market. You may have to charge less than you'd like just to stay competitive with other graphics businesses.

To get business, volunteer to do design for schools, churches, and other nonprofit organizations. Begin to build a portfolio of your work. Send out promotional flyers with marketing and business tips. Somewhere in the flyer, talk about the importance of well-designed business printed pieces and give your telephone number where they can get help in designing printed materials for their firm. You might even hold a seminar about well-designed business printing. Of course, once they are convinced they need to upgrade their business stationery, cards, and promotional pieces, you are right there to offer your services. In addition to all of this, contact businesses and get appointments to show your portfolio.

For more information, contact: The Graphic Artists Guild, 11 W. 20th St. 8th Floor, New York, NY 10011, (212) 463-7730.

Mailing List Brokers
Start-up cost: $1,500 to $2,500
Break-even: Six months to one year
Annual income: $10,000 to $75,000

List brokering requires a computer with a large disk storage capacity. It's a business that is continually in demand. It provides customers with three things:

1. *Capturing names for clients* from their invoices, receipts, and any other sources they might have. If a customer has come once to a client's business to make a purchase, he is the best possibility for another sale. By capturing his name

on a mailing list, it may be possible to encourage him to return to purchase more goods and services. A list of previous customers' names can be a gold mine for the merchandiser.

2. *Creating specialized mailing lists* such as lists of doctors, dentists, service people, or newcomers to your area. These lists can be sold to companies seeking contact names.

3. *Designing a direct-mail campaign* for your clients using names you have gathered into a mailing list. If you have not yet built a sizable list, you can rent names from other databases and concentrate your efforts on designing the direct-mail campaign for your customer.

You can charge a monthly fee for maintaining a client's list or for each direct-mail project or campaign you design and execute for your client. An average fee for entering a three-line name and address is $.15 per name. A four-line address would be $.20. An average fee for printing a label would be $.06 to $.08 each. Envelopes run $.10 to $.12 each. Charge extra for rush orders and for pickup and delivery. To avoid figuring all of this, you can charge $1 per year per name, so that if a client has 5,000 names, he pays you $5,000.

This is database management and you will be most successful if you have some experience. It is important that you also understand postal regulations that control mass mailings. Work in the field for a while to learn the business, take classes in database management, and talk with postal people about their regulations. They will be happy to walk you through different kinds of mailings. They want your mailings to be done correctly. It ensures your success and makes their job easier.

Business Writing
   Start-up cost: $1,500 to $2,000
   Break-even: One to six months
   Annual income: $40,000 to $100,000

There are several kinds of business writing and it will probably take several kinds to provide you with a full-time from-home business. Let's look at some types of business writing.

Resume Writing

One thing we can count on: Americans will change jobs every few years. Every time they do, they will need a new resume. For many people the preparation of a resume—that first-impression piece of paper—is a no-man's land. They just don't know where to start a resume, how long to make it, or when to end.

Many of them head straight for the yellow pages to find someone to help. A good resume writer tries to help the candidate isolate his or her very best traits and then present them in a logical fashion. Somehow the resume writer, who is also an interviewer, must find out what the person's best talents are and highlight them in the resume.

Resume writers can earn from $50 for a simple resume to $300 for a full curriculum vitae. Customers will include college students getting ready to enter the work force, young workers seeking to move up in their field, those who have not written a resume in many years, and almost anyone else who is seeking a job.

Business Plan Writer

A business plan is a road map for success. Many new businesses are started without one, but those with a business plan are more likely to succeed. As a business grows, a plan is essential for attaining loans, attracting outside investors, selling the business, or franchising the operation. Yet most business owners find this a tedious, fearsome task. They need help.

In order to help the business owner, you have to be able to see the business from his viewpoint, to hear his plans and dreams for the future, and be able to see the situation from the viewpoint of the investor.

You will need good grammar and writing skills and a background in business. You will need to understand good business writing (what a business plan looks like), and possess a high level of organization.

Fees range from $2,000 to $5,000 for each business plan. If you are an expert and have a large client with a complex business plan, you can charge up to $25,000 per plan. You can also agree to review a client's business plan after he has prepared it. For this, charge only a few hundred dollars.

Other Business Writing

In addition to resumes and business plans, business owners and business people often need manuals, annual reports, press releases, sales letters, critiques, direct-mail copy, and catalog copy.

To become trained for business writing, take business writing or journalism courses at a local community college or business school. You can also gain experience by working in an advertising firm or public relations office.

You can charge from $20 to $100 an hour for this kind of writing. If your client requires a lot of business writing, you can go on retainer for $1,000 to $2,000 per month.

Directories

Start-up cost: $1,500 to $2,000
Break-even: One to six months
Annual income: $20,000 part time to $60,000

You can put together directories for all kinds of goods and services. Perhaps one of the most interesting is a listing of artists, crafts people, art and craft shows, and local and regional businesses that deal in crafts. It can also include sources of supplies for the artist and crafter.

When assembling any kind of directory, choose the geographic area to be covered in the directory, then start your research. List a talent section, a services section, a sponsors' section, and a welcome section. All information is put into a computer and desktop published.

To offset the cost of printing, charge an advertising fee to each artisan, shop, and supplier listed in the directory. Think through your rates carefully, since this is your income from the project. Stress to your advertisers that they will receive free copies of the book to resell in their stores. Some of them will sell enough directories to repay the cost of their ad, besides attracting customers to their shop.

Contact libraries and arts-and-crafts councils and sell them copies for their reference sections. Set up at craft and art shows where you can sell copies of the book. If booksellers are reluctant to carry your directory in their stores, see if they will take them on consignment. If they do sell, the next time you come in with an armload of books, the bookseller will be happy to have your directories in his store.

This is a product that must be updated yearly and resold. If you've done a good job and produced a high-quality book, you will have no trouble selling next year's "new, improved, updated" version.

Dietary Analysis
Start-up cost: $1,500 to $2,000
Break-even: One to six months
Annual income: $30,000 to $45,000

I'm sure it's no surprise to you that our society has become extremely health-conscious. Restaurants know this, and many identify healthy items on their menus with a little heart or some other device. But there is a glitch. New rules by the Food and Drug Administration require that anyone making a health claim must be able to substantiate that claim.

Certain software programs have been designed for dietitians and are now available to consumers. With this software, you simply type a list of the ingredients into the "recipe" area of the program, then enter the serving size, hit the print key, and the computer will print a detailed nutritional analysis.

Your from-home work includes contacting area restaurants and offering to analyze their menus for nutritional value. National food chains probably have their nutritional analysis done for all of their restaurants. So look for non-national eateries. Don't rule out the local big-name restaurants. They may be the eating establishments *most* interested in your services. Contact publishers of cookbooks, authors of cookbooks, and health food restaurants.

Show prospective restaurant owner customers a printout of one of your favorite recipes. Remember, this analysis is not a one-shot deal. Restaurants frequently change their menus and those new food items will need to be analyzed for nutritional content before they make "healthy choice" claims.

Here are some computer programs to consider:

Diet Analyst from Parsons Technology
(800) 223-6925

The Food Processor from ESHA Research
(503) 585-6242

Health and Diet Pro for Windows from DSR Software
(800) 455-4377

In a small market, charge $35 to $50 per menu item and up to $150 to $200 in a city market. You could offer a fairly high per-menu item price or a package price for the entire menu. For a cookbook, charge $10 to $20 per recipe.

As I mentioned at the beginning of this chapter, there are thousands of applications for computer-based businesses and a new one is born every minute. Here are some more business ideas for you to research (there are dozens of books in libraries and bookstores on these topics) and consider based on your interests and skills:

> *Clip-Art Service*
> *Collection Agency*
> *Computer-Aided Design (CAD) Service*
> *Construction and Remodeling, Estimating, and Planning*
> *Service*
> *Coupon Publisher*
> *Creative Consultant*
> *Databased Marketing Services*
> *Diet and Exercise Planning Service*
> *Disk Copying and Translating Service*
> *Drafting Service*
> *Form Design Service*
> *Indexing Service*
> *Inventory Control Services*
> *People Tracing Service*
> *Property Management Service*
> *Proposal and Grant Writer*
> *Temporary Help Service*

The one area of computer usage we have not discussed in this chapter is that of using your home computer to do your current job from home. This from-home work is called telecommuting. In the next chapter we'll take a look at this rapidly growing field.

CHAPTER SEVEN

Telecommuting and the Information Highway

At 8:00 A.M. Monday morning Jerry goes to his home office. He's going to his job, but he sure doesn't look like it. He's wearing sweats and athletic shoes and looks like he's just come in from a run. He sits down at his computer and turns it on, logs on to his company's system, and begins to read his E-mail. No meetings today. He draws a deep breath and thinks, *Good! Now I can truly concentrate on the project Tom wants me to pull together for the meeting on Friday.* Jerry's week has begun and he is soon hard at work.

Sound like something you'd like to do? More and more people are finding ways to telecommute with their companies, and their companies are seeing the benefits of such an arrangement. Recently a group of my friends came to dinner. One of them had convinced her company she would be happier telecommuting. She now spends about 80 per cent of her time working at home and only goes to the office to pick up her mail and attend meetings. Not only is she happier, she is also more productive.

I attended a business conference about starting your own business and working from home. The instructor asked the audience what they most wanted to learn from the conference. The number-one desire was learning how to make more money; the number-two desire was to find more time—for family, friends, and for God (and service to him).

When the Los Angeles earthquake hit, roads were damaged beyond quick repair and a commute took three hours each way. Many people began telecommuting. For a couple hundred dollars these telecommuters purchased a modem—a device that transmits information over telephone lines. With a simple command, they logged onto their companies' systems and went to work.

How much time do you spend commuting to your job? One of the greatest benefits of the new information highway is not movies on demand or interactive home shopping but the ability to productively spend the time previously taken up with commuting to work in labor from home.

Let's take a look at this phenomenon brought about by technological advances that have begun to revolutionize the way we live.

COMMUNICATING ON THE INFORMATION HIGHWAY

Those who are building their own businesses admit to days of fear—"Can I make it?"; "I can't see very far ahead"; "I'm all right today, but what about three months down the road?" Those who telecommute for a company don't have these worries. Company benefits are in place, communication lines are open, and security is assured. It truly is the best of both worlds—you save time, get to wear leisure clothes, enjoy more productive work hours, and keep all the paid benefits of a regular job.

The companies that are allowing employees to work from home at least part of the week have drafted their own definitions of telecommuting.

Travelers Corporation, a $57 billion insurer, has been a trendsetter in this area. Its definition is: "Telecommuting is an individual working at home, supported by appropriate hardware, software, telecommunications and home office management and services."

CONVINCING AN EMPLOYER

Although telecommuting is growing rapidly, it is still the exception rather than the norm for most companies. Middle managers, upper-level management, human resource departments, and others are afraid of losing control of employees, and sometimes with good reason. Unfortunately, some telecommuters have abused the situation and have caused companies to have second thoughts about letting employees work from home. When an employer calls an employee's home and there is no answer to the call, and if it happens repeatedly, the employer begins to have suspicions that perhaps not quite as much work is going on as he expected.

When done with integrity, telecommuting is good, not only for the telecommuter but for the company as well. Here are some facts you might use to convince your employer that telecommuting would be good for your company.

1. *It would be possible for a company to use the same desk for two employees* whose schedules alternate days in the office and days at home. As far as being out of touch with the rest of the workers, there are now programs such as ISDN (integrated services digital network), and CTI (computer-telephone integration) that make it possible for two or more remote employees to work on the same material at the same time. If you were to type information into your computer using one of these systems, your coworker(s) could see it being typed. You can't be more in touch than that.

2. *It might mean that a company could keep a valuable, trained employee* when such things as a mate's move would

ordinarily mean a resignation. It could mean keeping some-one who for other reasons, such as the need to be accessible to an aging parent, might be able to keep a job if allowed to work from home.

3. *It saves the employer and the employee time.* Telecommuters admit that when they were in the office they used to walk down the hall to talk with coworkers only to find them on the phone, so they would go back to their desks and send them E-mail. If they were working from home, they would not even waste time walking to the coworker's office in the first place.

4. *It's possible to keep the same hours as in-house employees.* The employer needs to know that the employee will be on the job when all the other employees are. That's what works best. If the telecommuter is keeping the same office hours as his colleagues at the office, he is accessible to answer questions either by phone or E-mail, to be on conference phone calls, and to take phone calls or pick up voice-mail messages.

If the telecommuter's main office is on the east coast and he lives on the west coast, it could mean he must go to work at 5:00 A.M. to be on the job when his office is open. But just think about the long afternoons of leisure such a schedule would provide.

One study indicates that companies may save as much as $8,000 per telecommuter per year in increased worker productivity and reduced worker turnover. Retraining workers and waiting for their productivity level to rise is an expensive business. Some of the other benefits of telecommuting are:

- An enhanced ability to recruit and retain top employees.
- Reduced absenteeism.
- Reduced facility requirements at the central site.

- Increased professional creativity and productivity.
- Better off-peak use of its data center by telecommuters who elect not to work during nonbusiness hours.
- The corporate image-buffing that comes with its enhanced reputation as a leader in the innovative use of technology and human resources.

If you've discussed the possibility of telecommuting with your supervisor and he or she is still not convinced, here are some other ideas for getting him or her to try it.

- Tell him about other companies who are doing it. Use the information from Travelers' Insurance listed above.
- Ask for a trial period. You think you can accomplish more from your home. Perhaps you need to prove it.
- Ask to trade working from home for an annual raise. You will probably save more in commute costs, clothing, dry-cleaning, and lunches than you would have made from the raise.
- Ask to try it part time. Perhaps two days a week are what's needed to convince your employer of telecommuting's value.
- Tell him you will quit, but only if you are sure of your value as an employee. It's risky to threaten to quit unless you are serious. Someone might be waiting for the opportunity to take you up on it. Of course, if telecommuting is important enough to you, and your employer will not bend, you will probably want to quit anyway.
- Above all, move slowly. Give the system time to adjust and the employer time to get comfortable with a different way of managing people. Prove that you are more productive that one day a week or one day every other week when you are working from home.

AN AGREEMENT

After convincing your boss you need to telecommute, it might be a good thing to make an agreement between you so there are no surprises and no conditions not spelled out.

Brad Schepp, in his book *The Telecommuter's Handbook,* has a sample agreement with some very fine considerations that will help you understand some of the concerns of an employer. Here are some of those important points to consider.

- Employee salary, job responsibilities, benefits, and company-sponsored insurance coverage will not change due to participation in the telecommuting project.
- The amount of time the employee is expected to work will not change due to participation in the telecommuting project.
- For the purpose of defining the employee's job tour period, during which the employer has liability for job-related accidents or illnesses and during which worker's compensation laws apply, it is understood that the employee's work hours will conform to a schedule agreed upon by the telecommuter and his or her manager.
- If a schedule has not otherwise been agreed upon, the employee's work hours while telecommuting are assumed to be the same as before beginning to telecommute.
- Any changes or extension to the above-mentioned schedule with respect to worker's compensation coverage must be reviewed and approved by the employer in advance.
- Since the employee's home work space will be considered an extension of the company work space, the company's liability for job-related accidents will continue to exist during the understood and approved job-tour hours.
- A designated work space should be maintained by the telecommuter at the alternate work location. Worker's

compensation liability will be limited to this work space as opposed to applying to all areas of the home.

- As this liability will extend to accidents that may occur in the alternate location, the employer retains the right to make on-site inspections of this work area to ensure that safe work conditions exist.
- On-site visits by the employer may also be made for the purpose of retrieving equipment and other company property in the event of employee illness or termination.
- Any hardware or software the company purchases remains its property. Products developed while telecommuting for the company become its property.
- Company-owned software may not be duplicated except as formally authorized.
- Restricted-access materials (such as payroll) shall not be taken out of the main office or accessed through the computer at a remote location.
- Company equipment in a remote office shall not be used for personal purposes.
- The company will not purchase furniture or answering machines for telecommuters.
- The company will not provide custom-calling services, second phone line, printers, or personal computers to telecommuters.
- On a case-by-case basis, the company will consider partially reimbursing an employee for monthly service charges on a second telephone line and/or custom-calling services. Reimbursement, if approved, will be proportional to the amount telecommuted (one day a week telecommuting gets 1/7th of the bill reimbursed, and so on). This applies only to the service charges; the usage charges for, e.g., a second line, are dealt with below.
- Supplies required to complete assigned work at the alternate location should be obtained during one of the tele-

commuter's in-office visits. Out-of-pocket expenses for supplies normally available at the company will not be reimbursed.

- The company will not reimburse the employee for supplies such as computer paper, floppy disks, and cables.
- The company will reimburse the telecommuter for 60 percent of all company-related telephone calls.
- Expenses not specifically covered above will be dealt with on a case-by-case basis, taking into account the reasonableness of the expense, other expenses reimbursed for the same employee, and the overall budget for the project.
- Telecommuting is not to be viewed as a substitute for child care. Telecommuters with preschool children are expected to have someone else care for the children during the agreed-upon work hours.
- Individual tax implications related to the home work space shall be the responsibility of the telecommuter. It is possible, under some circumstances, to deduct expenses of a home office, but a tax expert should be consulted first.[4]

This agreement is only meant to be a boiler-plate, a place to begin to talk with your employer about working from home. If you were to present such an agreement to him, he would be convinced you were serious about taking care of his needs as well as your own and it would help to convince him that you understood his concerns about taxes, time, insurance, workmen's compensation, and a lot of other factors.

If you finally get the go-ahead to try telecommuting, keep in close touch with your office. Call often, go in frequently, watch for signs that communication is breaking down, and if you feel that it is, spend more time in the office and more time talking by phone to people in the office.

JOBS FOR TELECOMMUTERS

Suppose you've proposed the idea of telecommuting to your employer and gotten no response. Suppose you really do want to end the five-day commute and have more quality time with family. There are lots of jobs that lend themselves to telecommuting and you may have to seek one of them.

Most telecommuting jobs are white-collar jobs and have these things in common:

1. Telecommuting jobs do not require much face-to-face interaction.
2. Telephones and computers are the key tools used for the job.
3. Employee performance can be easily measured.
4. Telecommuting jobs do not require access to materials at the central workplace.

Here is a list of jobs that lend themselves to telecommuting:

Abstracter
Accountant
Actuary
Advertising copy writer
Advertising representative
Architect
Auditor
Bank officer
Book author
Booking agent
Bookkeeper
Budget analyst
Columnist
Computer service technician

Computer systems analyst
Consultant
Copyeditor
Correspondent
Cost estimator
Critic
Customer service representative
Data-entry clerk
Database administrator
Desktop publisher
Economist
Editorial writer
Educational consultant
Free-lance writer
Fund-raiser
Illustrator
Indexer
Information broker
Insurance claims representative
Legal assistant
Market research analyst
Medical records technician
News reporter
Pollster
Programmer
Public relations professional
Purchasing agent
Real estate agent
Records manager
Researcher
Reservations agent
Sales representative
Secretary
Social worker

Software writer
Speechwriter
Sportswriter
Stockbroker
Technical writer
Telemarketer
Transcriber
Translator
Travel agent
Typesetter
Urban planner
Word processor

When I look for books on telecommuting at the local library, I almost never find them on the shelves. That tells me there is a tremendous interest in the whole subject of working from home through the avenue of telecommuting.

Why shouldn't you be one of the innovative people who blaze a telecommuting trail for others in your company to follow? Are you weary of the commute, the business lunches, the endless meetings, the lack of productivity? Perhaps telecommuting is for you.

CHAPTER EIGHT

~ꞏ✥ꞏ~

Capital Ideas

There are thousands of franchise possibilities and thousands of people who are tired of being in a business some other person owns, or who have been forced out of those businesses by downsizing. They are now pursuing franchise opportunities.

Franchises encompass everything from tiny work-from-home operations to those requiring space in a mall. In fact, yesterday I was in our local mall and saw a kiosk that said something about "Business Opportunities." A pamphlet that was provided advertised franchise opportunities within the mall.

Some of the franchises available may be things you've never thought of, such as "Wheelchair Getaways," which is serving the booming market for van transportation for the handicapped and the mobility impaired. This makes it possible for elderly and physically disabled people to travel not just locally, but all over the world.[1] Or how about "Kitchen Tune-up,"[2] where the franchise operator refurbishes kitchens and offices by restoring existing cupboards and sometimes adding new ones? Just to show you the wide variety of franchises available, did you know that you can buy a company called "Shred-it"? The business of this company is on-site shredding of documents and paper recycling.[3]

In this chapter we'll choose a few of the many opportunities available for franchises and look at some resources for learning more about them. First, let's just talk about the whole idea of franchising—the promises, the pitfalls, the successes, and the dangers.

SO YOU WANT TO BUY A FRANCHISE

First of all, slow down. No matter what a franchiser offers, there is no easy money. Franchises require a lot of hard work to become successful, maybe even *years* of hard work. Think before you leap into a franchise operation.

To help you consider a franchise, hire a franchise lawyer. Franchise law is complicated and you need a specialist to help you through the franchise agreements and disclosure documents. To find a franchise lawyer, look in the yellow pages or get a copy of The Directory of Franchise Attorneys published by Franchise UPDATE Publications in San Jose, California. Also contact The Council of Franchise Suppliers, a unit of the International Franchise Association in Washington, DC.

Some questions to ask the attorney you finally select are:

1. What is your experience with this franchise or a similar one?
2. Have you ever represented this franchise, its competitors, or a franchise owned now or before by the same executives?
3. What will you charge?
4. Do you have a flat-fee service package which would give the basic advice and review the disclosure documents and agreement?
5. Am I important to you or will you shuffle me off to a junior partner?
6. May I see a list of your franchise clients?

A good franchise attorney should handle the following tasks:

1. Analyze franchise disclosure documents and agreements.
2. Evaluate if you should form a corporation and, if so, what kind.
3. Help you understand how you can use the company name in your business name. Under many franchise agreements you cannot use the company name or trademark and you must state something like "Franchise Unlimited, Inc. is doing business as Hopping Hosiery Company of Anytown, U.S.A."
4. Help with licenses and permits, especially if your product is environmentally sensitive.
5. Provide information or contacts with the franchise industry in general so that you can do your own investigation and questioning of other franchise owners.

You can also get some help from a CPA. A good one should be able to look over the franchiser's financial statements to see if the company has the resources to deliver on its promises and if you can make the profit you hope to make.

WHAT TO EXPECT FROM A FRANCHISE COMPANY

If, after hearing the cautions, you are still convinced that franchising is the way to go, then let's look at some of the things to consider before plunging in.

The most basic things to look for are:

- a strong and proven franchise concept
- a financially sound company
- a commitment to franchisees
- an in-place support system
- a thorough marketing program

Beyond these basics, there are some other considerations.

1. Pick a franchise that is interested in producing and selling *quality products*. You can have a wonderful marketing program and a snazzy presentation, but if the product is crummy, you'll not succeed. The franchiser must be interested in the satisfaction of the consumer—the end customer—and not just in making money himself, or even in seeing the franchisee make money. Some companies who care about the ultimate customer are Coca-Cola and McDonald's. Their quality products are developed with the customer in mind.

2. The franchiser should support the franchisee by allowing him to be the main distributor of a product in an area and not compete by owning or selling to stores in his area. Dunkin' Donuts allows the franchisee to sell donuts to quick-stop and convenience stores in his area rather than the parent company supplying the stores. This helps the owners of the franchises to increase their sales.

3. The franchiser should supply goods for which there is a market demand. The parent company must have more than a good idea. It must have products or services the public wants.

4. Choose a franchiser with a well-known trademark. If you choose one with a lesser-known trademark, you should not have to pay as much for the franchise, either in the initial fee or in royalty rates.

5. Think carefully about your franchiser's business system and marketing plan. These are at the heart of your future success.

6. Talk with some other franchisees in the system. Find out about their relationship with the franchiser. Is it supportive? What problems have they encountered? How were they resolved? Is collective bargaining part of the system? What

recourse will you have when treated unfairly or illegally? Collective-bargaining associations function essentially as labor unions.

7. Purchase a franchise that shows an attractive return on the investment. Work only with a franchiser who is willing to release sales and other figures to you. You have a right to know before you purchase your franchise.

8. Select a franchiser who supports the American Association of Franchisees and Dealers (AFFD) Bill of Rights. This gives the franchiser and the franchisee a negotiating list.

DANGER ZONE

The road to franchise success may be fraught with potholes and treacherous intersections. Before launching into such a venture you need to know the dangers.

A recent congressional hearing tackled the tough problems of franchises, and there is the promise of some continued hot debates in Congress on the subject. Some of the topics being discussed are the failure rate of the franchisees and deceptive promises franchisers make. What would you do if you'd invested $10,000 in a company and that company went belly-up before you'd had a chance to see a return on your investment? What would you do if you counted on the promises of the franchiser—that you'd make the $10,000 investment back in six months, or that in five years you'd be a millionaire and it failed?

My brother, Glen, has worked from home for many years. He's also tried a number of ventures, one of which was his own construction company specializing in remodeling. He bought a franchise that tied in with his construction interests. The franchise was a mobile carpet company.

What he bought when he purchased the franchise was a zip

code area in which he could sell, a panel van, carpet samples, a company name, and, supposedly, a support system.

When I asked him if he thought buying a franchise was a good or bad thing, he said that for him it was a bad thing. Because he was in a franchise, he talked with many other franchisees in lots of different kinds of businesses and found that few of them had good experiences unless they were buying a McDonalds or another franchise at that level.

He has decided that franchise companies are good at marketing their franchises but not at marketing their products. What they are good at is marketing a business system. The reason Glen had purchased a franchise was to get help with marketing. He'd had to market his construction business on his own and found it tough going. He was hoping to learn from experts how to do it. He pleaded with the parent company for help and they either wouldn't or couldn't give him any ideas about how to proceed.

Another key principle that should have been defined before Glen signed the papers (he learned after it was too late) was a definition of success. Glen's definition of success and the company's were entirely different. They considered a franchise making $25,000 a year successful. Their most successful franchise only made $45,000 per year. Deduct 15 per cent royalties from that, plus the cost of doing business, and see how much you have left. Not enough to live on, for sure.

A franchise looks like easy money, but the truth is, you'll work harder for that money than you might at a regular job. Glen concludes that the most successful franchises are those in which the owner is doing the work. If a franchisee has to hire someone to do part of the work—like installing the carpet you've sold—you have added expense and you do not have complete control of the quality of the finished job. Franchises like carpet cleaning, where the owner is also doing the work, tend to do quite well.

It is Glen's belief that if you think a franchise is a good opportunity, you should first ask yourself if you could achieve the same results without buying the franchise and paying the royalties. Could you start a similar business on your own? Then you would truly be working for yourself and not another company.

Here are additional dangers to be aware of before purchasing a franchise:

1. As a franchisee, you cannot sue a franchiser for violations of the Federal Trade Commission or state rules. Only a regulator of the FTA can sue and they are very slow to do so.
2. You would have more protection if you were buying stocks than if you are buying a franchise because the regulatory standards for franchises are inadequate.
3. You cannot be guaranteed that the promised earnings will come to you. Franchisers are notorious about making inflated promises of earnings.
4. If the franchiser fails—goes bad, changes hands, goes bankrupt, changes management, or even disappears—the franchisee has no escape. He is required to continue paying for something that no longer exists.
5. Some franchisers offer arbitration in the event of problems or failure of the franchise. Watch carefully, sometimes these are a smoke screen and the arbitration never happens.[4]

PROCEED WITH CAUTION

Now that I've thoroughly frightened you about ever investing money in a franchise, let me say that lots of people continue to buy into franchises and continue to do very well. There are sound opportunities available, and while you'll have to work very hard to make them succeed, if you make the right choice, you can make a good living and perhaps even do better than that.

Before signing on the dotted line, consider these questions:

- Do you have one year's living expenses set aside?
- Are you prepared to sacrifice time to make this business go?
- Are you prepared to do everything that needs to be done in the business?
- Is the franchise you've chosen something you already know? The most successful franchisers choose one that is close to the kind of work they've been doing.
- Will you have an office at home or a business office?

Income Opportunities[5] is a publication that can be very helpful to you if you are looking to buy a franchise. The magazine is issued monthly and always has a column about franchising. In addition, there are dozens of ads in each magazine for franchises. Each year the magazine features a survey of the top 200 franchises in the United States.[6]

Just for fun, let's look at some categories of franchise opportunities:

Copy centers	*Transportation of children*
Mobile furniture repair	*Food—restaurants of all kinds*
Sign making	*Baking*
Tub and sink resurfacing	*Home inspection*
Transmission specialists	*Lawn service*
Ceiling repair	*Maintenance and commercial cleaning*
Document shredding	
House cleaning	*Photography*
Car detailing	*Weight control*
Food delivery service	*Computer learning centers*
Auto rentals	*Yogurt shops*

Clothing and fashion shops
Sports equipment and clothing
shops
Vending machines
Tax preparation
Silk screening
Software companies
Managing mailing lists
Blinds cleaning service
Personalized books
Electronic equipment sales
Laser printer cartridge
recharging
Engraving service
Vinyl repair
Repairing cracked windshields
Countertop repair
Steel homes
Travel businesses of all kinds

Management recruiting
Nanny placement
Information brokering
Parking lot striping service
Temporary personnel service
Specialty foods marketing
Advertising specialty items
Antique sales
Catering
Collection agency
Coupon advertising mail service
Home/apartment prep service
Professional organizing
Personal fitness training
Carpet cleaning

These are only a few of the many franchise opportunities available. A couple of franchises I spotted were truly innovative and caused me to say "Huh?" I would rank them in the "too good to be true" category. One was a coupon business where customers buy only the coupons they want for products they normally purchase. The initial investment of the franchisee was under $300 and the franchiser promised only a "limited number of distributors in an area to maximize the profits for each distributor."

The other one fooled me with its lead—"Own your own cash machines." I thought that meant someone had thought up the idea of operating their own automatic teller machine, but the truth is, it is a vending machine for personal products. So pay attention to the print—especially the fine print—in the ads.

FINDING FRANCHISE SUPPORT

Of course, one of the key elements of a franchise situation is that the franchiser is supposed to give lots of support, which means you should be able to call someone in the franchiser's office for information about marketing, quality of products, answers to questions your customers ask, positive input about how your business is progressing, and answers to any other questions you many have. But is there a way to know which franchise is best for you? How do you get started?

Some of the obvious ways are to talk with franchise owners about their successes and failures. Talk with them about the pitfalls they have encountered and what they would do if they were starting over.

Do your homework. Read entrepreneurial publications like *Inc.* and other money magazines. Scour the library for books about franchising and read them diligently.

I spotted a couple of other ideas from ads:

1. Attend a franchise exposition where all kinds of franchisers have their wares and services on display. Watch for these fairs in your area, or write to International Franchise Expo, 1133 Louisiana Ave. Suite 210, Winter Park, FL 32789.
2. Learn the secrets of small-business success while taking a Caribbean cruise. This cruise is sponsored by *Income Opportunities* magazine and is on a well-known cruise line.

If, after all I've said in this chapter, you still think buying a franchise is the solution to your work-from-home business; if you have sufficient capital not only to invest in the franchise but in the marketing you need to get you started; and if you realize that when you own a franchise you are still working for someone else, then go for it, and I wish you well.

CHAPTER NINE

Catalog Cash

Mail order isn't such a new idea. A hundred and twenty-one years ago Aaron Montgomery Ward mailed one-page merchandise flyers to his customers. It cost him about $1,500 to do it. That was a lot of money in those days. He was then joined by Sears Roebuck. Since that first flyer, people across the country have eagerly awaited the seasonal arrival of catalogs. Today, our mailboxes are flooded with specialty catalogs—selling everything from writing paper and pens to seed catalogs to storage boxes and containers. Ward's first flyer has exploded into thousands of catalog companies resulting in well over a $200 billion business that shows no sign of slowing down. The New York-based Direct Marketing Association (DMA) projects a growth rate of up to 15 percent each year for the next five years in catalog sales.

Start-up cost: From $100 to $100,000, depending on what you are selling and how much inventory you are stocking
Break-even: Two months to two years
Annual income: A few hundred dollars part time to $70,000 as a full time job

Millions of buyers now shop from the convenience of their own homes, at their own pace, and in their own time. Mail-order houses have made delivery and return very simple. Toll-free numbers and the use of credit cards eliminates the need to send in an order or even write a check. So mail order and catalog shopping have become a powerful economic force in this country.

THE LILLIAN VERNON WAY

Lillian Vernon was a young pregnant homemaker when she took $2,000 of her wedding gift money and began her catalog business on her kitchen table. Today that business is worth $196 million.

You can start small. Lillian did and so did L.L. Bean and a seven-year-old company called Levenger—a home-library niche catalog company. Small can be good. It can be personal. Customers want to be treated well and a small mail-order company can do that.

When choosing a name for your company, keep it simple, descriptive, and easy to remember. Susie's Country Gifts is an easy name to remember and it tells right away what kind of products you will find in the catalog. Bill's Auto Accessories is also easy to remember and descriptive of the catalog's contents.

Your customers, however, don't need to know that you're operating off the kitchen table. Make your print material professional looking and attractive. Your catalog or flyer is your image. And forget the word *mail order* in any piece of literature. That says "kitchen table" and not an established, here-to-stay company.

Attractive doesn't necessarily mean full-color and slick. It can be a black-and-white line drawing kind of catalog and still be highly effective. Good black-and-white photos work very well. Keep it personal by showing pictures of you fulfilling customer orders, and make sure your catalog letters to customers are warm and friendly and have a handwritten signature at the bottom.

If you don't have desktop publishing capabilities, go to a local quick-print shop. Often a print shop will have someone trained in desktop publishing who can produce a fine-looking piece for you. Just remember to keep the personal touch in design and copy.

EVERYBODY'S DOING IT

Mail order is a broad term for selling products or information by mail. The products you sell can be either your own or those of other manufacturers.

All kinds of things are sold by direct mail—everything from recipes to correspondence courses, from clothing to bee-keeping kits. What do you want to sell by mail order? Is it unique? Is it something customers truly want? Can you make them want it?

Where are your customers? What are they reading? That's where you want to place your first ad. Of course, you realize there is no mail-order business without advertising. Are your customers reading the *Wall Street Journal, Better Homes and Gardens, Country Living, Popular Mechanics,* or *Organic Gardening?* That's where your ad belongs.

Success or failure of your mail-order business probably will have little to do with the product you are offering, unless it is such a strange product that no one wants it. It will have everything to do with the advertising about your product. The right words, the way they are put together, the manner in which they address the potential customer's needs, all contribute to the success or failure of your venture. Ask yourself, "Do I know what motivates my customers to buy?" Your answer had better be yes if you want to succeed as a cataloger.

BEFORE *YOU* DO IT

Here are some things to consider before you leap into the mail-order business.

Research the market. Before you begin, do your homework. What is the product you intend to sell? Where are you going to get your supply? What is your competition? What is unique about your product? If it is not unique, why would the customer buy it over a similar product?

Understand your customers. Who are they? Why would they buy your product? What age or ethnic group are you aiming at? How are you going to find your customers?

Learn as much as you can about the business. Go to the library and read, read, read about mail order. Build a reference library. Get your name on other companies' lists to receive their regular mailings. Some of them are paying big, high-powered firms in New York to design their packages, and you can borrow ideas for free.

Be patient and hang in there. It's going to take time to build a business, and it's going to be hard work. But once you've decided on your product and produced and mailed your catalog, you will begin to receive returns. That's the fun part. Success is the result of trial and error, of learning from your mistakes. Keep going.

SPOT A TREND

If an idea or product comes on the market and is gone within a season, it was a fad. But if that same idea or product comes and stays and begins to grow, it is a trend. Changes in eating styles, the exercise craze, and skateboarding and in-line skating are trends that have changed our culture. It will never go back to what it was before these things came along.

One of the best ways to spot a trend is to read voraciously. Read popular magazines such as *People*. Read newspapers such as *USA Today*. Read specialty magazines such as *American Demographics*, a magazine that specializes in identifying trends. Pay attention even to home decorating, gardening, science, and mechanics magazines. Anything that you begin to see again and again could be a developing trend.

Trends often come in the wake of technological development. While technology may destroy old ways of doing things, it also provides many opportunities. Watch for new ideas. Be one of the first to catalog new products for the developing technology.

Just think about computers. Twenty years ago they were something only big companies and government agencies used. No one dreamed that someday most of us would own a computer and wonder how we could live without it. The computer industry created thousands of spin-off products and applications, with more to come all the time.

Right now, if you can think of some kind of lowfat food that hasn't already been created, you might be able to sell it in abundance. People are deeply concerned about what they put into their bodies and yet they don't want to give up all the good-tasting things to which they are accustomed. If you could invent a lowfat cookie that tasted as good as a Mrs. Field's original chocolate-chip cookie, you'd be rolling in dough—so to speak. (Of course, you'd have to find a way to ship the cookies so they didn't break or go stale.)

THINK ABOUT "THE LOOK"

You've spotted a trend. You've developed a product to match that trend. Now it's time to think about the look of the product and your advertising pieces. This is called "packaging." If you are marketing something inexpensive, take care with the packaging. A good-looking package convinces buyers of a quality product.

Packaging is the "makeup" of your product. Are you ever surprised when you see some of the world's most glamorous models before they apply makeup? I am. They look like ordinary women. Makeup transforms them. Your packaging can make all the difference in the world to your product's attractiveness.

That goes for your mailing pieces as well. Some ads look like an ad for a garage sale with everything all jumbled together. There are ads in the newspaper I won't read because they're cluttered. I don't shop at the places they advertise either.

What kind of impression do you want to put forth—classic elegance, friendly country, efficient modernity, organized professionalism, curious entrepreneurialism, rough-and-tumble outdoor enthusiasm? Only you know what market you are trying to reach and what appeals to that audience. The rough-and-tumble outdoor enthusiast will be totally turned off by classic elegance. The efficient modernist will gag at the country approach.

Can you see how important it is to know your audience? To be sensitive to their needs and interests? The other day I received a catalog for dog lovers. Now, I'm a dog lover, but I don't have a dog, and I thought, *I'm not even going to look at this. Well, maybe I'll just see what they could offer me if I had a dog.* Soon I was browsing through the catalog. I discovered they had lots of items for a dog or a dog owner, but they also had jewelry with dog motifs, sweaters with pictures of dogs knitted in, and I realized that I didn't have to have a dog to purchase from this catalog. That's smart merchandising.

THE AD

The heart of mail order is the advertisement. Everything starts with the ad. With a well-written ad you can sell almost anything. It doesn't have to be a full-page newspaper or magazine ad. Once again, small ads in the backs of magazines can be highly effective. Ads that are one column wide and two inches high are visible enough and not too expensive. For about $500 you can place a small classified in several magazines that will reach millions.

If your ad has a visual sameness month after month, it becomes highly identifiable. I purchased a pencil-post bed from just such a consistent ad in the back of a home decorating magazine.

Check for ads that run from month to month. If you see the same ad appearing over and over, you can be sure it is working, and that's why the company continues to run.

Don't try to include everything in your ad. Simply say, "Write for more information," or "For more details write...," or "Call this toll-free number." When I first wrote to the company that makes the pencil-post beds, it was more out of curiosity than of being certain I would buy. They sent me, in response to my call to a toll-free number, a full-color flyer. You couldn't call it a catalog because there wasn't that much to it.

The primary purpose of a classified ad is to attract qualified buyers. When they respond to the ad, then you can follow up and send a friendly letter and descriptive literature. The material you send should be an expansion of your original ad. It should tell the benefits of your product. It should provide all the information the customer needs to decide to purchase the item.

The most important part of the package is the letter, which should begin with, "Thank you for answering my ad." This is your one-on-one piece, your friendly introduction to your company.

Here's an effective classified ad I spotted recently:

READ "How to Write a Classified Ad That Pulls." Instructive booklet tells how to write an effective classified ad. Also, includes a certificate worth $5.00 toward a classified ad in this publication. For your copy, send $4.75 (includes postage/handling) to: 10 PUBLICATIONS, INC., 1500 Broadway, Suite 600, Dept. CL, New York, NY 10036 (Allow 4-6 weeks delivery.)[1]

This one-inch ad gives you all the information you need. You know what you are buying—a booklet; you know what it's about—writing effective classifieds as demonstrated in this classified; you know how much money to send—$4.75, which includes postage and handling; you know there is a bonus—a $5.00 gift certificate toward placing an ad; you know exactly where to send your check—New York; and you know how long it will take to get the booklet—4 to 6 weeks.

Do you see how important advertising is? I contacted the bed company because I saw their ad over and over again. I called them because they had a toll-free number. I looked over their flyer for a long time and did nothing. It was when I received their second mailing that I purchased.

In both cases—the bed and the booklet—a well-written classified ad did the job. I picked them out of all the others on a page that had fifty-six classified ads. I will send for the booklet, because I want to know what advice these people give.

An ad larger than a classified does have its good side. It says to the buyer, "Here is a credible company. This is no fly-by-night operation." Now, that may or may not be true, but in the mind of the ad reader it is probably the case.

So, how do you get a good ad? If you have a little talent for writing, try writing it yourself. After you've written the ad, take it to an editor or copywriter for fine-tuning. It will be fairly inexpensive if you've pulled it together first.

If the whole idea of writing an ad overwhelms you, consult with an ad agency and ask them to give you several ideas. Remember that just because they are professional ad writers doesn't mean they would do a better job than you, and they are fairly expensive, charging anywhere from $20 to $100 per hour. You know your product better than they do; you should know your customers better than they do; and you have the passion for selling the product. So don't take the first ad copy a writer offers you just because you think that person knows what he or she is doing. When you see the finished copy, ask yourself if this is truly the image you want to project about yourself and your product. Did the ad writer capture the essence of you and your company? Is this how you want to approach your customers?

Take the ads the writers produce for you and test them. Take them to a shopping mall and ask several shoppers which one they would respond to more quickly. Ask friends, relatives, and anyone else who will listen. Very quickly you'll get a feel for what works and what doesn't.

William Bond, who writes on the subject of mail order business, says the ad must have an AIDA (Attention, Interest, Desire, Action) approach. Let's look at those four elements.

Attention—This is in the headline and it says "You're a special person."

Interest—This tells why the customer should be interested. You have the answers to his interests. You have the solution to how to get from being interested in your product to owning it.

Desire—You'll show him the benefits of buying your product. You'll show him how his life will be better because he's buying your product. You'll make promises to him.

Action—You'll ask him to take action—fill out the reply card, write a check, mail the card.[2]

After the ad is written, either by yourself or someone else, test its effectiveness by asking questions:

1. Do you have a central idea?
2. Do you describe your product or service clearly?
3. Is it believable?
4. Do you show how your product is different?
5. Have you used the AIDA formula?
6. Do you ask for your order?
7. Do you tell them how to take action?
8. Would you order the product or service after reading this copy?
9. Is it exciting enough to get the order for you?[3]

Again, an excellent way to learn which ads work and why is to study lots of ads. Watch for those that appear consistently month after month. Ask yourself what about the ad catches your attention. Analyze the component parts as listed above.

- Are all the component parts there?
- How do they capture your attention?
- How do they keep your interest? Do they make you want the product? How?
- Do they use a picture?
- Do they make a promise?
- Do they ask you to take action?
- Do they ask you to fill out a postcard?
- Do they ask you to call a telephone number?
- Do they ask you to call a toll free number?
- Is there a coupon in the ad?
- Is the ad appropriate to the magazine or newspaper in which it appears? (If it's a gardening magazine, is the product somehow related to gardening?)

HOW MANY PEOPLE WILL YOU REACH
WITH YOUR AD?

If you are going to spend money for advertising, and you must to develop a mail-order business, it's important to know how many people you're reaching with your ad. An inexpensive ad in a paper or magazine that reaches 20,000 people may in the end be more expensive than a costlier ad that reaches 300,000 readers.

Magazines that advertise have a rate card for various sizes and shapes of advertising. You can receive a rate card by writing to the magazine's advertising department. Somewhere on the rate card you will find the magazine's circulation—the number of people who receive their magazine or newspaper. When you have the rate for the ad you've chosen and the circulation figure, it's pretty simple to figure out what it will cost to reach each reader. (In the advertising business it's figured as "cost per thousand." What will it cost to reach 1,000 people?) By comparing several magazines, you'll soon be able to see which ad is the best buy. Even though the cost of the ad may be a little higher, consider how many people you are reaching and it won't seem so bad.

When you finally run your ad in a magazine or newspaper, put some kind of code on it so you'll know which ad your customers responded to. A department name like Dept. USA might tell you the ad was run in the *USA Today* newspaper, or use a code number like CL-1-96 to indicate the ad was run in *Country Living* magazine in January 1996. Of course, you can only keep track of these responses to different ads if something, such as a coupon, is mailed back to you for ordering. If your orders are being taken by phone, the person who answers the phone will have to ask where the buyer saw the ad and if there is a code number on the ad. Use a different code for each ad and keep track of the responses. This will tell you which magazine or newspaper works best for your product.

PRODUCT AVAILABILITY

In the catalog business, you can't send out your catalog and then get the product after you've received responses from your customers, unless you know you can get the product on the same day, and that is highly unlikely. You must have at least some product on hand and you have to know that you can get more product quickly if your ad works better than you had anticipated. If you were selling something manufactured in Asia, it might be several months before you could have stock on hand to fill orders.

If you do run out of a product, you must notify your customers immediately. Orders you cannot fill are called "back orders" and they are expensive because you must notify the customer of the delay. That means someone has to spend time writing letters (which means extra money) and you have to pay extra postage (even more money) for that contact. If a customer ordered several items and only one of them is not available, that item will have to be shipped individually, which also adds to your postage cost. And there is always the possibility the customer will cancel the order because he or she doesn't want to wait for the product.

In the mail-order business you will have to invest in at least some inventory to fill the orders before you get your first order. You will also need a place—a warehouse—to store your inventory. In the beginning this can be a garage or basement, but if your business grows as you hope it will, you'll soon be looking for warehouse space. While you can run the office from home, you'll probably have to rent warehouse space to store the product.

You will need some system of keeping track of inventory. In the beginning you'll be able to write down each shipment, but soon you'll want to put inventory on a computerized system—a data bank—for tracking.

You will also need an order form, unless you are using a classified ad. The best way to find out which order forms are most user-friendly is to order catalogs and study their enclosed order forms. What makes the most sense to you? What looks the most appealing? Which one would you be quickest to use? You don't have to reinvent the wheel, just copy the one that seems best to you and try it out. In the beginning it doesn't even have to be printed; it can be produced on desktop publishing and photocopied.

There are, as you can see, some complications, but the potential to make a lot of money from home is also in the mix, because there is no middle man. You don't have to sell to a retailer at a discounted price. You can charge the customer the going retail rate and keep the discount in your pocket. You also have no overhead for a retail store, and you can specialize in products that wouldn't sell enough to support a shop. You don't have to wait for your customer to come to your shop to show them what you have, you can go to them. Bad weather won't keep people from buying. In fact, it might help because they can simply fill out an order form or call your toll-free number to order instead of going out in a blizzard.

And while there are some start-up costs, they are probably lower than for any other business. One author says that thousands of people have started mail-order businesses with less than $100. He was one of those people. All of the products he sold were on consignment or were purchased in such a way that they could be paid for after the sale. He then plowed all his profits back into the company. He spent money on ads, stationery, envelopes, postage, and an answering machine. The only other money he spent, in the beginning, was to register his business name.[4]

The other wonderful thing about mail order is that you can do it in your spare time in the beginning. You don't have to quit your day job. In fact, it would be wise not to quit your day job until you have your mail-order business up and running.

FOUND DOLLARS

A profit side of the mail-order business that novices don't consider is renting your list to other mail-order companies. Lists are rented all the time, and if you don't believe me, order something from a mail-order catalog and misspell your name. Before long you will be getting catalogs from all kinds of companies with your name misspelled.

You will need to have several thousand names on your list—20,000 or more—before you are ready to rent it. Renters will probably take only 5,000 names the first time to test whether your list is responsive to their product. If it is, they'll be back for more names and a full "roll out," a term which means the renter of the list rolls out a mailing.

The money earned from list rental is gravy. All you have to do to earn it is provide labels to the renter. Renters cannot steal your customers. They can only use your list one time. The customers they gain from your list will be those who buy from them. For that reason, you may choose not to rent your list to competitors. Or you may choose not to rent your list at all. But if you do rent it, it's easy money.

In order for your list to be effective, you will have to keep it clean. You do that by paying an extra fee to the post office when you mail and asking for updated addresses. I moved recently and my catalogs did not follow me for three months, but all of a sudden I am receiving them again. The post office has notified the catalog companies of my whereabouts and they are faithfully mailing again.

THERE'S HELP

We're not going to be able to go into much more detail about mail order in this book, because my purpose here is to introduce you to possible ideas for working from home and not to describe them fully. For more information, check out the Resources section at the back of this book and get started with your own research on mail-order businesses.

CHAPTER TEN

Setting Up Your Workplace

Once you've strategized your business, you'll know how to set up your workplace and how much space you will need. If your business is mail order, you'll need shelves and storage for your products and an area to package and ship the product. You'll also need a desk and equipment for accepting, keeping track of, and billing customers—if you choose to bill customers rather than have them send payment with the order.

If your business is gift baskets, you'll have to store the bulky baskets and all the component parts, along with ribbons, fabrics, and shredded plastic grass or other decorative filler materials. You'll also need packaging material to ship the baskets, if you are selling them mail order.

If you are going to work from a home computer, your setup will need an ergonomically correct desk and chair for the long hours you'll spend sitting. Buy the best and most comfortable chair and desk you can afford. If you are an editor or a writer, you'll need all of these items plus bookshelves for research books and the mountains of paper that accompany the writing-editing business.

If your from-home business requires that you see clients in your office, you'll need to have something that looks more like an office than a corner of a bedroom. An outside entrance to the office would be best, if possible.

If you are a consultant who will be working mostly in other people's offices, you can do with a very small work space in your home. If you are a traveling salesperson, you will need some space but not a lot of it. If you are an artist, you won't need an office, but you will need a studio with a certain kind of lighting and quite a bit of room.

Before you jump into setting up an expensive office, consider your needs carefully. Do you really need an office? If you are working outside your home as a consultant or salesperson and only basing your business from home, perhaps the kitchen table will do. Maybe all you need is a file cabinet tucked away somewhere and a shelf for office supplies. In the beginning, it is of utmost importance to keep costs down and profits up, and one way to do that is to not have an office with expensive equipment and furnishings. Setting up an office can be fun and can make you feel like you are really doing business, but think before you act.

For all kinds of businesses these days, you'll need a telephone and a fax machine and probably a computer. The best option is two telephone lines, one dedicated to the telephone and the other to the fax. This avoids confusion for your customers. You may also need a modem for transmitting information to your office if you are telecommuting. Once again, a dedicated business line will be helpful for transmitting information by modem. That leaves your information and order line open for other uses. In any office setup you'll need proper lighting, heating, cooling, and file storage.

If you are using your home phone lines for business, talk with your telephone company about custom ringing. A distinctive kind of ring will identify whether the incoming call is personal or business.

IT DOESN'T HAVE TO COST AN ARM AND A LEG

Sound expensive? It is a little, but let me tell you how I set up my workplace inexpensively.

Since I'm an editor and writer, I'm one of those people with lots of books, magazines, and papers to file. When I tried the free-lance route for a while, I purchased a folding table from a wholesale house for about $30. This is my work table and desk. It is three-by-six feet and provides a good-sized area for all my stuff. The drawback is that it has no drawers in which to file projects or even pencils and paper clips. And it looks messy all the time.

The desk is too high for my computer. If I were to put my computer and keyboard on it at that height, it would exhaust my arms and shoulders and probably cause injury. I went to a secondhand store and bought an old-fashioned typing table, the kind with the drop-leaf wings. I made sure I got one that was sturdy and wouldn't loosen in the joints the first time I used it. It is just the right height and it only cost $5.

For a while I had my books and magazines in the closet of the bedroom I use for an office. I had them in plastic milk crates stacked up like bookshelves. I'd purchased the milk crates for $1.25 at a local thrift shop. That was only marginally successful because the crates were too flimsy for the weight of the books.

So, I soon found a furniture store going out of business and bought three seven-foot oak bookcases with six shelves in each one. These shelves now hold my needed books and supplies. They cost me $60 each for a total of $180.

While I was living in Seattle, I went to the Boeing surplus store to shop for a metal file cabinet. This is a place where the overflow of the huge Boeing aircraft manufacturing company is sold. There you can find everything from upholstery fabric used in airplanes to file folders to desks, lamps, and rubber bands. I found a five-drawer steel cabinet with a security lock bar attached. It was perfect for my needs. I stashed it out of sight in the closet. It cost an amazing $65. The chair I'm sitting on also came from Boeing many years ago. It cost about $35.

The stand that holds my fax machine is actually a sturdy low bookshelf on wheels. I bought it at a garage sale for $10.

I ordered the fax machine from Damark in Minneapolis. Damark is a clearinghouse for overstocked goods of all kinds and has a lot of electronic equipment. My computer also came from Damark and cost me one-third what it would have if I'd bought it retail.[1]

Other furnishings in the room are a wicker basket for a wastebasket purchased for about $1 at a thrift store and a fan-backed wicker chair salvaged from a Dumpster at an apartment where I lived for a short time. The chair came with a cushion I covered with a pleasing fabric. Wall decorations include a huge photo of a rose that I took. An end table—a reject from one of my decorating adventures—holds the telephone and answering machine.

My workroom works for me. It is used for nothing else. I come here each morning for a couple of hours to write and sometimes in the evenings to pay my bills. When I walk out of this room, I walk away from this phase of my work and go to my job, to my housework, or to some fun activity. I don't think about this phase of my work again until I'm ready to come back into the room.

I'm not satisfied with the table-for-a-desk arrangement and so I'm watching secondhand stores for an old-fashioned oak desk that is not too large and is in fairly good condition. (I don't want to do a lot of refinishing. The prices run from $75 to $150, and most of them will need some kind of work to make them fully operational and attractive.)

Another thing to think about is the colors you use in your

office. If you're serious about from-home work, you'll be spending a lot of time in your office. Research says that colors have a physical effect on us. Red increases blood pressure and is associated with energy and stimulation. Yellow is a bright, happy color. Blues and greens give a relaxed atmosphere, reduce blood pressure, and suggest tranquility. A nationwide travel franchise dictates the color schemes of its outlets—blue, green, and wicker white. One can see the rationale of the franchise's color choices. The agencies are hoping to encourage people to take long, relaxing vacations in a wonderfully tranquil place.

Avoid blacks, browns, grays, and earth tones. These colors are associated with fatigue and sedated behavior and they make your office seem smaller. Of course, white or off-white expands size and is not at all unobtrusive or distracting.

Remember that money spent fixing up your office is tax deductible.

FIND A PLACE FOR AN OFFICE

I didn't always have an office. I've worked at the kitchen table, in a corner of a bedroom, and any other place I could spread out my books. Having a place to work, a place dedicated to your from-home job, is important. When looking for a home, if you plan to work from home, office space should be high on your list of priorities for a house, apartment, or condominium. It doesn't have to be very big or very fancy, but there must be a place to spread out work and leave it at least for a few hours.

Both of my brothers started their businesses in their homes. They had the luxury of room in the basement to set up offices and they both had walkout basements with entrances. Each brother had a support person working with him to do invoicing, routine correspondence, and to answer the phone. One of my brothers still works from home, the other is in roofing and owns a huge warehouse with offices where materials, equipment, trucks, and lots of other necessities for his business are stored. His business outgrew his home long ago.

If you are serious about working from home, you'll have to find a place for an office. My father, a wise blue-collar philosopher says, "Build the barn and the barn will build the house." In other words, take care of business first and the rest will follow. Perhaps in the beginning your workplace will be no more than a space in the living room or dining room. Maybe it's a converted attic over a garage, or maybe it's a chunk carved out of the garage itself. Maybe it's a walk-in closet. As your business grows you'll need more space and more equipment to organize your work space.

When you think you've found a spot for your home office, here are a couple of considerations:

• Will there be enough storage space or room to build storage space?
• Will the office be accessible to the services you need, such as copying, typing, messengers?

Although laws and rules have been tightened by the IRS, there are still deductions for home offices if the room is used only for an office, and if you are earning a substantial part of your income from that office. Check with your accountant for the specifics. Not only can you take the floor space deduction, but a portion of your heat, electricity, and security system (if you have one). You cannot take telephone service unless you have a business line. Residence lines don't count. But you can deduct toll calls made for business purposes. So keep careful records of toll calls and to whom they were made. You can do this right on your toll call record on the phone bill.

WHAT ABOUT THE LITTLE STUFF?

Let's take a look at the little necessities—letterhead, business cards, paper clips, and lots of other miscellaneous items.

- Stationery—As soon as you've decided what your from-home work/business will be, and have chosen a name, at least get business cards printed. If possible, get letterhead and matching envelopes printed as well.
- Business cards are inexpensive and are important because they become a memory-tickler to a prospective client. The client looks at your card, sees its design and quality, and sticks it in his pocket. Later he pulls it out—maybe not until the jacket is headed for the cleaners, but he finds it—and he remembers.

  If possible hire a graphic designer to design your business logo and stationery. It may cost a little more, but it is well worth it to have a smart-looking logo and one that is memorable.
- Mailing and labeling materials. You'll need envelopes of various sizes and kinds—like padded envelopes, stamps, and labels.
- Binders—You may need binders for storing copies of letters from clients, schedules, and lots of other stuff.
- File folders—You can purchase file folders in a rainbow of colors and use them for various kinds of projects or parts of your business—clients' correspondence, schedules, projects, ideas, along with any other pertinent information you need to keep in a file.
- Miscellaneous—You'll need tape of various kinds, a stapler and staple puller, paper clips, and rubber bands. You'll need an organizer of some kind to hold all of this stuff and it's best if it can all be put in a drawer rather than on top of the desk. You may want a bulletin board or a scheduling board of some kind.

Tips for an Efficient Office

- Buy in bulk whenever possible. There's usually a discount for quantity purchases.

- Buy stamps in bulk because it saves time.

- Shop thrift stores for office supply items.

- Reuse office supplies as much as possible.

- Set up a briefcase desk if you travel a lot. Stock the briefcase desk with invoices, cards, note pads, pencils and pens, envelopes, stamps, and anything else you might need during a presentation or a trip. You can grab what you need on the way out the door without having to search for items.

- When you find something that saves you time, consider buying it. Time is one of the most valuable items you have.

Equipment List for Your Office

- ☐ Telephone
- ☐ Answering machine
- ☐ Computer and/or typewriter
- ☐ Fax
- ☐ Modem
- ☐ Safe

Shopping List for Office Furniture

☐ Desk
☐ Chair
☐ Wastebasket
☐ File cabinet(s)
☐ Extra chair(s)
☐ In and out baskets
☐ Bookshelves and other storage.
☐ Clock
☐ Bulletin board
☐ Work table
☐ Radio
☐ Fan or air conditioner
☐ Lamps
☐ Art to hang on walls
☐ Pencil and pen holder

Supply Checklist for Your Office

☐ Pens
☐ Pencils
☐ Erasers
☐ Typing paper or computer paper
☐ Typewriter correction paper or fluid
☐ Scratch pads
☐ Memo pads
☐ Paper clips
☐ Rubber bands

- [ ] Stapler and staples
- [ ] Scissors
- [ ] Tape—clear and mailing tape
- [ ] Tape dispenser
- [ ] Brown paper for wrapping packages
- [ ] Stamps
- [ ] Envelopes in several sizes
- [ ] Mailing labels
- [ ] Clipboard
- [ ] System for storing names, addresses, and telephone numbers
- [ ] Files
- [ ] Filing supplies
- [ ] Small file boxes for index cards
- [ ] Typewriter or printer ribbons
- [ ] Business card holder
- [ ] Desk organizer
- [ ] Glue
- [ ] Hole punch
- [ ] Letter opener
- [ ] Paper clips
- [ ] Pencil sharpener
- [ ] Postage scale
- [ ] Ruler
- [ ] Rubber bands
- [ ] Three-ring binders

TAKE INVENTORY

You don't have to purchase everything at once, even though you'll want to. However, make sure to take an inventory of all your office equipment and furnishings for insurance purposes. Here's what you need to do:

1. List each item in your office, the year it was purchased, its original cost, and its present value.
2. List the model number, brand name, dealer's name, and a description of the item—or take a photo.
3. Store the inventory in a safe place apart from your office, such as a safe deposit box.
4. Update the inventory regularly.

What's Important to Office Workers

Item	% of workers considering it to be "very important"
Good lighting	.88
A comfortable chair	.73
Good circulation of air	.70
The right temperature for you	.69
Machines and reference material within easy reach	.69
The opportunity to stretch and move around during the day	.67
A place to work when you need to concentrate without distractions	.63
Enough space to move at your desk	.57
Quiet	.53
A window	.40
A place where you can go to relax	.38
The ability to change your office furniture as your job changes	.24[2]

Setting up a workplace is one of the most enjoyable parts of setting up a from-home work situation. It is a small but important part of the process. For more help, refer to the Resource section in the back of this book, then search the library or the business section of a bookstore for ideas about how to set up your workplace. Business magazines frequently have articles about the office, your desk, handling papers with efficiency, and lots of other helpful information.

CHAPTER ELEVEN

Getting the Support You Need

You gotta have friends and you gotta have support—especially if you are working from home. One of the biggest enemies of from-home work is isolation—loneliness. Some people love it, some people hate it, but both kinds of from-home workers need contact with the outside world to find clients and vendors, to learn new trends in business, to find solutions to problems, and just for general support.

Here are some of the things a from-home worker will miss after leaving the workplace:

- Inside information—the kind which is casually dropped at the beginning of a meeting or at a coffee break.
- The feeling of being part of a group—of belonging somewhere.
- The social pressure that encourages you not to snack all day long and, instead, to get out for a walk.
- Moral support in the face of an emergency.
- A place to try out a new idea.
- Encouragement from coworkers to keep going.
- Someone to complain to.
- Someone to confront you when you're headed in the wrong direction with a project.
- Self-esteem building when you're planning a new project or when you've done a project well.
- A sense of importance that comes with being needed by an organization.

Networking and support are tough to come by when you are working alone at home. You can have the support you need, but you'll have to work at it. Here are some ideas for building support.

THE INNER CIRCLE

Family. The most important support group for someone working from home is family. We've already talked a little about bringing your family into the planning stage of starting your business, but ongoing support from them is vital. Does your spouse know what you are doing and that it takes time to do it? Does your spouse know this is hard work and that establishing your own business is more than a little scary? Help your family see what you are trying to accomplish, that it will take time to accomplish it, and that you will have to spend time working at it like any other job. You will not be available to pick up clothes from the laundry, get the car lubed, or attend afternoon ballgames any more than if you were working in an office downtown.

Do your children understand that you are working, even though you don't go out to an office, factory, or other workplace? Do they understand that your goals for your business will eventually benefit them? Many women decide to establish a from-home work situation to avoid paying for child care. Unfortunately, it doesn't work like that. Most from-home workers need to hire child care, at least part of the time. Otherwise, the business will suffer and may eventually fail. You have to be available to take calls from clients, report to your main office, be available for conference calls (if you are telecommuting), and get out to meet vendors. If you are trying to care for your children without help, either the child will suffer from neglect or your business will.

There is a good side to this, however. Little children nap and won't need more than a quick check on them periodically. Some from-home workers let their little ones nap in a playpen right beside them. Older children are in school at least part of the day. The rest of the time, instead of taking them to a high-priced daycare center, it is possible to hire a high school student to spend time with them. He or she might even start dinner for your family. And if there is a crisis, you are right there to handle it.

Children need to learn respect for your workspace. If your business involves the use of tools, they are off-limits. If you have a gift basket business, the children are not to take ribbons to wrap a gift. If you use a computer, they are to keep their hands off. Your work space must be respected, even if it is only a corner of your bedroom. If you are in your workplace, working, your kids need to learn to leave you alone.

The beauty of working from home is that it offers flexibility. Suppose your toddler needs Mom in the morning; you can spend that time with him and work later into the evening that day. When school-age children come in from school, they're usually ready for a snack and a chat. When they are fresh from their school experience they are ready to talk about it. After they get involved in homework or are out playing, they forget to tell you how their day went. How great if Dad would plan his afternoon break time around the arrival of his children from school!

Extended Family and Friends. Family and friends may be the biggest violators of your time. It may take a firm hand and a firm voice on the phone to convince them you are truly working and are not available for chit-chat. Stay tough, they'll get it after a while. Tell them about your goals and accomplishments so they, too, can support what you are doing.

THE NEXT RING

After your family, the next most important people to support you are your accountant, your attorney, and other free-lance people who provide services you need.

Accountant. Unless your from-home business is accounting, you'll probably need an accountant to help you avoid the snafus and pitfalls of IRS regulations. Maybe you'll only need year-end bookkeeping preparation for taxes; maybe you'll need full bookkeeping services—someone to issue invoices, keep bank accounts straight, and do other general bookkeeping tasks. Depending on the size of your from-home business, this person could work on your accounts once a week, twice a week, or on a daily basis.

If you need only the quarterly or yearly services of an accountant, you will need to set up a system for filing papers and documents so they are readily available to the accountant. You will take care of sending invoices, banking money, and the daily financial aspects of your business.

Attorney. It's good to have someone to go over contracts, guide your general business decisions, and talk through problems that might have legal ramifications. An attorney should be someone who has training or experience in handling business matters. A personal attorney is probably not the best person to handle your business matters.

Free-lancers. You will need the help of other free-lancers in order to get your business done. These free-lancers could include graphics designers, printers, advertising specialists, secretaries, computer experts, and a host of others, depending on what your business needs. Look for quality results from your free-lancers, and when you find people who do the kind of work you want, stick with them. In fact, you can sometimes reduce costs by contracting with your free-lancers to do all your work with them or by putting them on retainer. Often when the free-lancer is guaranteed work he can reduce his charges to you.

THE SMALL BUSINESS ADMINISTRATION

Perhaps one of the oldest and best-known networking and support groups is the Small Business Administration (SBA). This is a government agency with all kinds of help for small-businesses. The government is very supportive of and friendly toward small businesses. Perhaps the government understands that small businesses built this country. In the last few years, many of the new companies started in this country were begun as small businesses and many of them were built by women.

According to U.S. government statistics, the number of small businesses has increased by 54 percent since 1980. These businesses also account for 50 percent of the private work-force, contribute 44 percent of all sales in the country, and are responsible for 38 percent of the gross national product.[1]

The SBA provides an organization known as the Service Corps of Retired Executives (SCORE). SCORE provides counseling, training, and information services. This puts you in touch with a retired executive in your field of work to give you support. These are people who have been through the process you're going through and they understand the ins and outs of establishing a from-home business.

After you have followed the SBA's recommended procedure and written a business plan, know where you want to operate, know how much cash you will need to get started, and have specific information on employee, vendor, and market possibilities, you may want someone to look over your plan with an objective eye. It's time to call a SCORE representative. These representatives can be reached through the Small Business Administration. The SBA can also review your plan and help with fine-tuning. These helps and supports are free; use them.

Another service provided by the SBA is the Small Business Institute and Small Business Development Centers. Call the SBA for more information. There is a Small Business Administration office in nearly every major city in the country, and if you are not in a major city you can call SBA's "Answer Desk" at 1-800-368-5855. (See more information in the Resource section of this chapter.)

While you are on the phone with the SBA, ask for their Directory of Business Development Publications. These are the pamphlets and booklets mentioned in chapter 1. Here is a sampling of the material available:

Financial Management and Analysis
ABC's of Borrowing
Profit Costing and Pricing for Manufacturers Basic
Budgets for Profit Planning
Understanding Cash Flow
A Venture Capital Primer for Small Business
Accounting Services
Analyze Your Records to Reduce Your Costs
Budgeting in a Small Service Firm
Sound Cash Management and Borrowing
Recordkeeping in a Small Business
Pricing your Products and Services Profitably
General Management and Planning
Effective Business Communications
Locating or Relocating Your Business
Business Plan for Small Manufacturers

Business Plan for Small Construction Firms

Planning and Goal Setting for Small Business

Should You Lease or Buy Equipment?

Business Plan for Small Service Firms

Checklist for Going into Business

How to Get Started with a Small Business Computer

The Business Plan for Homebased Business

Small Business Decision Making

Inventory Management

Techniques for Problem Solving

Selecting the Legal Structure for Your Business

Evaluating Franchise Opportunities

Crime Prevention

Curtailing Crime—Inside and Out

A Small Business Guide to Computer Security

Marketing

Creative Selling; The Competitive Edge

Marketing for Small Business

Is the Independent Sales Agent for You?

Marketing Checklist for Small Retailers

Researching Your Market

Selling by Mail Order

Market Overseas with Government Help

Personnel Management

Checklist for Developing a Training Program

Employees: How to Find and Pay Them

Managing Employee Benefits

New Products/Ideas/Inventions

Can You Make Money with Your Idea or Invention?

Introduction to Patents

The cost of these pamphlets and booklets averages about $1 each. This is the finest, most well-thought-through information available for a person starting a business.

PROFESSIONAL NETWORKING GROUPS

Professional networking groups abound. For instance, there is an organization known as LeTip. The sole function of this organization is networking. After a continental breakfast and a short (about ten minutes) motivational talk, participants spend a few minutes talking with each other, swap business cards, and go their way. The whole point of the organization is to get referrals. Each member is expected to supply at least four referrals a month, but most members provide more.

Each LeTip group averages about forty professionals. In essence, these people become your sales force and your customers. Every time you interact with one of them, you interact with the whole sphere of people in their network. It's like dropping a pebble in a pond. The rings in this case are circles of people, and the circles are ever-expanding. For more information, call 1-800-25LETIP.

Another group is the National Strategic Alliance Network of Entrepreneurs (NSAN), a division of Charles J. Givens Business Success Institute. Joseph L. Sgarlata is the principal founder and creator of the NSAN.

The organization's mission is to empower individuals to achieve personal and entrepreneurial excellence. The NSAN offers an array of programs and specialty business opportunities and franchise opportunities. The organization brings financial clout, negotiation, consultation, and marketing skills to even the smallest one-person, home-based business.

The organization's services fall into three main areas:

- Services needed to start your business (or to make a slight course correction). Includes creating logos and business cards, obtaining a merchant credit account, writing a business plan, valuating existing businesses and bookkeeping, among others.
- Services needed to operate your business on an ongoing basis. Includes long-distance services, business travel, equipment leasing, and recruitment.
- Services needed personally as the owner of a profitable, growing business. Includes personal tax deduction reviews and asset protection reviews to protect the wealth you build.

The NSAN structures its program for entrepreneurs and investors of every experience and income level. You will be assigned a personal consultant (a support person) who is only a phone call or fax away, twelve hours a day, five days a week, and even for a few hours on Saturdays.

I attended one of their free workshops and was given two books: *Local Business Information Kit* and *IRS Secrets, Shortcuts, and Savings*. These would be very valuable tools for anyone launching a from-home business.

Watch your newspaper's business section for this type of seminar or workshop. Or call NSAN in Florida at (407) 774-6656.

Be assured that once you attend a seminar such as this one, you will have information on many more such opportunities finding its way to your mailbox.

Your newspaper can be a source of many other opportunities for networking at all levels. Watch for them in the employment section of the newspaper. For example, here are some that were listed in a metropolitan newspaper:

- Tailor-made Marketing for Home-Based Businesses
- Successful Interviewing: How to Sell Yourself in the 90s
- 50+ Employment Opportunities Job Club
- Medical Billing Services as a Home Business

All of the associations and groups listed above are support groups that relate to from-home work.

INFORMAL NETWORKING

Perhaps one of the most valuable kinds of networking is the informal kind. Time shared with business colleagues, other from-home workers, and vendors can bring information, support, and encouragement to the from-home worker. Here's how to make the most of your most natural source of support.

1. *Establish a support group of people you know who are working from home.* I grew up in a small town in Montana where I worked as a telephone service representative. On work days, about three in the afternoon, my boss would disappear and be gone for about an hour.

I knew where he had gone because it was the same place all the businessmen in town went at three in the afternoon. My mother also worked in a business in town and her boss went there, too. Where did they go? The local drugstore that had a soda fountain and booths in the back. Talk about a networking group! Talk about a support group! Those men knew everything that was happening in town and they knew every business transaction taking place in the county.

If I go back to that little town today at three in the afternoon, I'll find men assembled not in the drugstore anymore—they took out the booths and the counter—but somewhere else in that town, leaning over their coffee cups, discussing cattle prices, weather, crops, who's buying what, the latest car models, the local sports heroes, and who knows what else.

That's support, that's encouragement, that's ready information. You as a from-home worker also need support, a network, a group who understands. Maybe you could arrange to meet some colleagues at a coffee shop once or twice a week to catch up on the latest business news.

2. *Take advantage of unexpected opportunities to network.* The story is told that Lillian Vernon, the great cataloger, was once stuck with several people in an elevator in a large office building. One of the women in the elevator was the owner of a toy company. As a result of their conversation while trapped, the toy manufacturer became a major supplier of toys for the Vernon catalog.

Ann Richards, former governor of Texas, went to ballgames to sit with the late Congresswoman Barbara Jordan. They talked business over popcorn at half-time.[2]

You can probably tell a dozen stories of your own about how informal networking has paid off for you or someone you know. Just being interested in others and what they are doing with their lives is a most valuable tool for growing a business.

A CO-OP FOR SUPPORT

Establish a co-op for support as well as economic benefit. Co-ops lend themselves particularly to those businesses with a product to sell. Crafts, antiques, basket-businesses, tailored items, and woodwork projects are sometimes easier to produce than to sell.

One group of handcrafters who established a co-op found a store to rent that had been vacant for some time. All of the participants got together, painted the place, and set up their displays. They had a lot of fun getting the place ready, but at the same time they were building a support group—a network.

While most of these women produce their goods at home, they have a place to get together and sell the goods. Not every woman has to be in the store every day. There is a schedule that frees them to do more work at home and spend more time with their families. What a wonderful way to build a support system.

OTHER WAYS TO FIND SUPPORT AND KEEP IN TOUCH

Support systems are not built automatically. They are built one relationship at a time. No one knows your need for support—for a network—unless you reach out and tell others. Here are a few suggestions to start your network.

1. *Join community, professional, technical, or trade organizations.* You are not alone. There has been a proliferation of home businesses over the past few years. There are associations just for home-business entrepreneurs. Find them on the Working from Home Forum on CompuServe.

One obvious way to benefit from such associations is to regularly attend the meetings. But an even better way is to volunteer within the organization.

2. *Read business and trade journals to keep in touch.* There are dozens of niched publications to keep you abreast of every new development of your business. Subscribe to a couple and read them.

There are also cassette tapes on every aspect of business and business relations. If you drive a lot for your business, it's a perfect time to listen to tapes. You'll find them advertised in all business magazines and in airline magazines.

3. *Use the telephone and E-mail to keep in touch.* Talk with friends and business acquaintances to get a reaction to a new idea, to hear their opinions, or just to share some news. Consider calls from strangers as an opportunity for new ideas and a way to broaden your network.

4. *Reach out and touch by means of an electronic bulletin board.* If you have a computer and are linked to a network, throw out a tough business question and wait for answers from all over the world. Browse through others' messages and questions and see if you can help a friend. After all, networking goes both ways.

You'll be talking on-line with people who are in the trenches of from-home work every day. These are the people who know how tough it can be. These are the people who've been there—done that—and have the answers.

On-line you can get almost the same kind of support and networking you would in an office.

5. *Take a from-home colleague to lunch.* Take a work-from-home colleague out for a meal. Or you might even have them come to your home. Yes, it breaks up your work day, but it also builds your network.

6. *Have people come to your office and go to theirs.* Are you afraid these people are competitors and will steal your ideas? I doubt it. In the writing business, we find that if we assign a topic to ten people and tell them to write a story or article, we come up with ten different stories, because each person writes it differently. No one will run his or her business the way you run yours, even if you both start with the identical information.

It makes sense to put away contractual information and schedules for projects before you invite others in, but be assured, you will gain more than you lose by getting together with business competitors.

7. Start a networking group. Can't find a networking group in your town? Start one. I am starting a novel writing club for a group of writers who have written many books but have never written novels. We know of no such group in existence, so we're hoping to push each other to produce several novels within the group in the next year.

TIPS FOR STARTING A NETWORKING GROUP

1. *You start it.* Somebody has to take the initiative. That somebody can be you. I'm starting the novel-writing club because I see value in it and I have the time, and no one else is taking the initiative.

2. *Let everyone know what you are up to.* When I got the idea for the novel writing club, I talked with a couple of colleagues who were enthusiastic. They told others and I have no idea how many will ultimately be involved. You never know who might want to be a part of your networking group, so talk about it. `

3. *In the first meeting, make it clear what the group is about.* In our first meeting we set the goals of the group, gave assignments, and made it very clear we were here to write, to produce novels, and not just to talk about it.

4. *Believe that every person who comes has a valuable contribution to make.* Anything less than this becomes self-serving.

Each person who attends will bring a valuable perspective on working from home. Listen carefully. What that person says may be the springboard to solve your problem.

5. *Decide if you want this to be a one-time or continuing event.* Staying in touch may be important to all of the group members. Our novel-writing club will meet once a month. That should give members time to do the assignments we give each other. A regularly scheduled meeting is easier to remember, and once a month is not too intrusive on family life.

Decide at your first meeting how often you will meet and where. Decide how large the group can be to remain effective, if visitors are encouraged to come, and if you need some kind of dues to cover postage and mailings.

NETWORKING RESOURCES

Groups and Associations

American Home Business Association
397 Post Road
Darien, CT 92619-7050

Leads Club
P.O. Box 24
Carlsbad, CA 92008
(619) 434-3761

LeTip International, Inc.
4907 Morena Blvd., Suite 13
San Diego, CA 92117
(619) 581-2400

Mother's Home Business Network
P.O. Box 423
East Meadow, NY 11554

National Association for the Cottage Industry
P.O. Box 14850
Chicago, IL 60614

National Association of Women Business Owners
1337 K. St. N.W., Suite 637
Washington, DC 20005
(301) 608-2590

National Association of Home-based Businesses
10451 Mill Run Circle, Suite 400
Owings Mill, MD 21117
(410) 363-3698

NSAN
1200 West S.R. 434, Suite 300
Longwood, FL 32750
(407) 774-6656

Small Business Administration (SBA)
To find the office nearest you, call (800) 827-5722 or write
to:

Small Business Administration
409 Third St. S.W.
Washington, DC 20416

Ask about their Service Corps of Retired Executives (SCORE) or write to:

Service Corps of Retired Executives
409 Third Street S.W.
Washington, DC 20416

Newsletters

Barbara Brabec's Self-Employment Survival Letter
P.O. Box 2137
Naperville, IL 60567
Subscription Price: $24 a year. Send $6 for a sample newsletter.

HomeWork
P.O. Box 2250
Gresham, OR 97039
Subscription Price: $20 per year.

HomeWork is a quarterly newsletter written with a Christian perspective for people who own a home or family business or would like to.

A wise person once told me that others will not know what our needs are unless we tell them. Life is not a guessing game where one person needs support and encouragement and others are supposed to know when to give it and why. Reach out. Build your own network; if you do, chances are good that you will never feel alone in your home business again. And even if you do, you will know where to turn for support.

The New American Dream

What is the American dream? Once it was a chicken in every pot. Then it was two cars in every garage. Then it was corporate ladder-climbing and incredible "me-ism." But what is the new American dream?

I think we got a clue when William Bennett's *Book of Virtues* hit the best-seller list and stayed there for a long time. We got a clue when all of a sudden the words "family values" became a standard line in all political speeches (whether in a positive or derogatory sense). We got another clue by statistics that tell us women are leaving the workplace, some after a hard-fought battle to gain position and acceptance in their fields, and going home to raise babies.

People have a great desire for family, home, traditional values, church involvement, marital commitment, and the opportunity to nurture their children. Unfortunately our economy does not always allow a family to exist on one income, and we have many single parents who must work or starve. So here is the tension: to be home where one can create an environment for raising children who espouse our faith and our values and to make enough money to meet family needs. How can we do both?

Perhaps finding a way to make a living from home is the answer. Perhaps that's why there are so many people turning toward home. Perhaps that's why so many new businesses are being started by women from their homes.

As Christians we need to step back and look at our lives. What are we trying to accomplish when we pursue high-paying employment that takes us away from our families for days on end? What do we gain when we are so tired and stressed from our jobs that we ignore or lash out at those we love? Is the job worth it, or could we, perhaps, find a way to earn a living that enhances family life, that draws us together, that causes parents to be there when those precious moments of opportunity for training and teaching present themselves.

I have not always been a working woman. When my children were young, I was a full-time mom. I was, however, almost the only full-time mom in the neighborhood.

I used to watch a couple of young teenagers who lived in a house behind ours. They would come home from school about 2:30 or 3:00 P.M. It was obvious they were bored and looking for some excitement. They would take tennis balls, cover them with lighter fluid and ignite them. Then they'd throw the burning tennis balls onto the cedar shake roofing of their house and watch the balls roll off.

Another group of unsupervised teens two or three houses up the hill would toss eggs into neighboring yards and onto the siding of the houses.

I began to wonder who was raising America's children. It looked to me as if they were raising themselves. I understood that one mother of those teens was a single mom and had to work. Another had just bought a fancy house and had to work to pay for it. And I understood that my choice to become a free-lance writer and stay home with my kids meant they didn't have the latest designer jeans or the biggest house. But they did have love and attention and help with homework problems. There was someone there to hear their funny stories from school and to bind up both physical and emotional wounds. They knew they were not going to be allowed to hang out at the neighborhood video joint. They would practice their musical instruments, get their homework done, and help with chores.

It seems to me that working from home is the best of everything. It provides the income the family needs, the oversight and care children need, and teaches them that money comes from labor and does not fall off of trees into their never-ending bag of wants.

I think it is wonderful if dads can find a way to earn money from home. Kids need their dads as much as they need their moms. They need dads who are there for them not just in body, but who are emotionally involved as well. They need a spiritual leader who isn't in such a rush to get to his next appointment that he has no time for prayer, Bible reading, or answering the hard questions of life from a biblical perspective. Working from home may provide a family with a much needed spiritual leader.

It is my hope that within the pages of this book you have found an idea that would make it possible for you to work from home. I pray that you will give serious consideration to finding a lifestyle that enhances family life. I trust you will find the information I have presented helpful and informative. I've written not to tell you what to do, but to spark ideas that might be the answer to your from-home work desire. This book comes with a prayer that God will guide you and your family as you launch upon the exciting adventure called "working from home."

INDEX OF IDEAS

NOTES

ONE

Is Working at Home Right for Me?

1. From an advertisement for Mary Kay, 1991, 1992.
2. Maggie Mahar, "A Change of Place," *Barron's*, March 21, 1994, 33-38.
3. Mahar, 33-38.
4. Gilbert Fuchsberg, "Female Enrollment Falls in Many MBA Programs," *Wall Street Journal*, September 25, 1992, B-1.
5. Anne Studabaker in "Inside View," *Profiles*, January 1994.
6. George L. Church, "Jobs in an Age of Insecurity," *Time*, November 22, 1992, 34-39.
7. Church, 34-39.
8. David Werner, in an article by Jan Yager, "If You're Fired," *Parade*, May 31, 1992, 16.
9. Marsha Sinetar, *Do What You Love, the Money Will Follow* (New York: Dell Publishing, 1987), 57.
10. For more information about work styles, read: Cynthia Tobias, *The Way They Learn* (Colorado Springs: Focus on the Family, 1994).
11. Adapted from Bobb Biehl, "To Be Your Best," *Broadcast News*, February and March 1993. Bobb Biehl is the president of Masterplanning Group, International. The phone number is (800) 443-1976.

TWO

Making a Plan

1. Mary Rowland, "Do You Have What It Takes to Start Your Own Business?" *Family Circle*, March 10, 1992, 76.
2. Donna Partow, *Homemade Business* (Colorado Springs: Focus on the Family, 1992), 54-56.
3. Rowland, 74.
4. Partow, *Homemade Business*. Used by permission of Focus on the Family.

THREE

Simple Work-from-Home Ideas

1. Based on information from Kathleen Gleaves, "A Blooming Business," *Income Opportunities*, n.d.

2.   Charles R. Whitlock, *How to Get Rich* (Chicago: Contemporary Books, 1991), 226.

FOUR
From-Home Ideas That Require Equipment

1.   Sharlene Fast, "Try Peggy's great treats," *The Mountain Villager,* April 15, 1993.
2.   Paula Nichols, "The Fruitful Gourmet," *Income Opportunities,* August 1994, 56.

FIVE
Craft Ideas to Earn From-Home Dollars

1.   Barbara Bartocci, "Make Big Dollars at Home," *Family Circle,* April 28, 1995, 56.

SIX
*Using Your Computer for Your
From-Home Business*

1.   "The Today Show," January 2, 1995.

SEVEN
Telecommuting and the Information Highway

1.   Brad Schepp, *The Telecommuter's Handbook* (New York: A Pharos Book, A Scripps Howard Company, 1990), 52.

EIGHT
Capital Ideas

1.   For more information on Wheelchair Getaways, call 1-800-642-2042.
2.   For more information on Kitchen Tune-Up, call 1-800-333-6385.
3.   For more information on Shred-It, call 1-905-855-2540.
4.   Robert L. Perry, Franchise Editor, "The Battle of '95," *Income Opportunities,* December 1994, 70-72.

5. Order *Income Opportunities* from P.O. Box 55207, Boulder, CO 80321-5207. Subscription rate: $17.99.
6. For more specific information on Platinum 200 Franchises, see the February 1995 issue of *Income Opportunities.*

NINE
Catalog Cash

1. Ad appearing in "Classified Marketplace," *Income Opportunities,* April 1985, 111.
2. William J. Bond, *Home-Based Mail Order* (Blue Ridge Summit, Penn.: Liberty Hall Press, 1990), 61.
3. Bond, 61.
4. Alan J. Falkson, *Make Money and Be Your Own Boss without Much Capital,* (Bayswater, Western Australia: Elaphas Books, 1993), 45.

TEN
Setting Up Your Workplace

1. Damark Corporation, 7101 Winnetke Ave. N., P.O. Box 9437, Minneapolis, MN 55440-9437. Phone: 1-800-827-6767.
2. *Income Opportunities,* P.O. Box 55207, Boulder, CO 80321-5207.

ELEVEN
Getting the Support You Need

1. *Extra Income,* February, 1994, 63.
2. "Weird Places to Network," *Working Women,* August 1992, 41.

RESOURCES

ONE
Is Working at Home Right for Me?

Germer, Jerry. *Country Careers: Successful Ways to Live and Work in the Country.* New York: John Wiley and Sons, 1993.

Kahn, Steve. *How to Run a Business Out of Your Home. Inc.* Magazine's Success Library. Stamford, Conn.: Longmeadow Press, 1987.

Kahn, Steve. *How (and Where) to Get the Money to Get Started. Inc.* Magazine's Success Library. Stamford, Conn.: Longmeadow Press, 1987.

Kishel, Gregory. *Dollars on Your Doorstep.* New York: Wiley, 1984.

O'Conner, Lindsey. *Working at Home.* Eugene, Ore.: Harvest House, 1990.

Partow, Donna. *Homemade Business.* Colorado Springs, Colo.: Focus on the Family Publishing, 1992.

Sinetar, Marsha. *Do What You Love, The Money Will Follow.* New York: Dell Books, 1987.

Van Oech, Roger. *A Whack on the Side of the Head—How to Unlock Your Mind for Innovation.* New York: Warner, 1988.

TWO
Making a Plan

Bangs, David H. *The Business Planning Guide.* Dover, N.H.: Upstart Publishing Co., 1992.

Bangs, David H. *The Start Up Guide: A One-Year Plan for Entrepreneurs.* Dover, N.H.: Upstart Publishing, 1994.

Pinson, Linda and Jerry Jinnett. *The Anatomy of a Business Plan.* Out Your Mind, 1989.

THREE
Simple Work-from-Home Ideas to Consider

Aslett, Don. *Cleaning Up for a Living.* White Hall, Va.: Betterway Publications, 1991.

Barrett, Linda. *Personal Services.* New York: F. Watts, 1991.

Editors of *Entrepreneur* Magazine. *184 Businesses Anyone Can Start and Make a Lot of Money.* New York: Bantam Books, 1990.

Feingold, S. Normam and Leonard G. Perlman. *Making It on Your Own.* Washington, D.C.: Acropolis Books, Ltd., 1987.

Edwards, Paul and Sarah. *Working from Home.* A Jeremy P. Tarcher/Putnam Book. New York: G.P. Putnam's Sons, 1994.

Gorder, Cheryl. *Home Business Resource Guide*. Tempe, Ariz.: Bluebird Publishing, 1989.

Kahn, Sarah and the Philip Lief Group. *101 Best Businesses to Start*. New York: Doubleday, 1988.

Paradis, Adrian A. *Opportunities in Cleaning Services Careers*. Lincolnwood, Ill.: VGM Career Horizons, 1992.

Partow, Donna. *Homemade Business*. Colorado Springs, Colo.: Focus on the Family Publishing, 1992.

Rizzo, Michael R. *How to Make Profits with Service Contracts*. New York: American Management Association, 1987.

Sattler, Helen Roney. *Dollars from Dandelions*. New York: Lothrop, Lee & Shepard, 1979.

FOUR
From-Home Work Ideas that Require Equipment

Gallagher, Patricia C. *For All the Write Reasons*. Worcester, Penn.: The Young Sparrow Publishing, 1994.

Holtz, Herman. *Computer Consulting on Your Home-Based PC*. Blue Ridge Summit, Penn.: Windcrest, 1993.

FIVE
Craft Ideas to Earn From-Home Dollars

Bandel, Gabriel. *How to Market and Sell Your Crafts*. Washington, D.C.: Bandele Publications, 1993.

Brabec, Barbara. *Creative Cash*. Naperville, Ill.: Barbara Brabec Productions, 1991.

Front Room Publishers. *Marketing Crafts through a Home-Party System*. Palm Beach Gardens, Fla.: Success Publications.

Gerhards, Paul. *How to Sell What You Make: The Business of Marketing Crafts*. Harrisburg, Penn.: Stackpole Books, 1990.

Long, Steve and Cindy. *You Can Make Money from Your Arts and Crafts*. Palm Beach, Fla.: Success Publications, 1987.

Oberrecht, Kenn. *How to Open and Operate a Home-Based Craft Business*. Old Saybrook, Conn.: The Globe Pequot Press, 1994.

West, Janice. *50 Ways to Sell Your Crafts*. Fort Worth, Tex.: The Summit Group, 1994.

Wheeler, Geoffrey. *How to Succeed in Crafts*. New York: Hobby Publications, 1973.

SIX
Using Your Computer for Your From-Home Business

Chandler, Marsha Kee. *Homegrown Computer Profits*. White Hall, Va.: Betterway Publications, Inc. 1989.

Edwards, Paul and Sarah. *Making Money with Your Computer at Home*. New York: Tarcher/Putnam, 1993.

Friedberg, Ardy. *The Computer Freelancer's Handbook: Moonlighting with Your Home Computer*. New York: New American Library, 1984.

Lis Flemming Electronic Cottage Handbook, Nos. 1 and 2. Davis, Calif.: Fleming Ltd., 1988 and 1989.

SEVEN
Telecommuting and the Information Highway

Davidow, William H. and Michael S. Malone. *The Virtual Corporation*. New York: Harper Business, 1992.

Gray, Mike, Noel Hodson, and Gil Gordon. *Telecommuting Explained*. West Sussex, England: John Wiley and Sons, Ltd., 1993.

Newsletter. *Telecommuting Times*, P.O. Box 142, Cheltenham, PA 19012.

EIGHT
Capital Ideas

Foster, Dennis L. *The Complete Franchise Book: What You Must Know (and Are Rarely Told) about Buying or Starting Your Own Franchise*. Rocklin, Calif.: Prima Publications, 1994.

Jones, Constance L. *200 Best Franchises to Buy*. New York: Bantam, 1993.

Perry, Robert L. *50 Best Low-Investment, High-Profit Franchises*. New York: Prentice Hall, 1994.

Purvin, Robert L. *Franchise Fraud*. New York: Wiley, 1994.

Tomzack, Mary E. *Tips and Traps When Buying a Franchise*. New York: McGraw-Hill, 1994.

NINE
Catalog Cash

Bond, William J. *Home-Based Mail Order*. Blue Ridge Summit, Penn.: Liberty Hall Press, 1990.

Cohen, William A. *Building a Mail Order Business*. New York: Wiley, 1991.

Falkson, Alan J. *Make Money and Be Your Own Boss without Much Capital.* Bayswater, Western Australia: Elephas Books, 1993.

Holtz, Herman. *Starting and Building Your Catalog Sales Business.* New York: Wiley, 1990.

Schultz, Marilyn Smith. *Mail Order on the Kitchen Table.* McAllen, Tex.: Tribute, 1988.

Simon, Julian Lincoln. *How to Start and Operate a Mail-Order Business.* New York: McGraw Hill, 1987.

Tepper, Ron. *Secrets of a Successful Mail Order Guru: Chase Revel.* New York: John Wiley and Sons, 1988.

Wilbur, L. Perry. *Money in Your Mailbox.* New York: Simon & Schuster, 1993.

Magazines:

Extra Income: P.O. Box 543, Dept. AS103, Mt. Morris, IL 61054.

Income Opportunities: P.O. Box 55206, Boulder, CO 80322, has a monthly column on Mail Order.

TEN
Setting Up Your Workplace

Alvarez, Mark. *The Home Office Book: How to Set Up and Use an Efficient Personal Workspace in the Computer Age.* Woodbury, Conn.: Goodwood Press, 1990.

Better Homes and Gardens Working at Home. Des Moines, Ia.: Meredith Corporation, 1985.

Faux, Marian. *Successful Free-Lancing.* New York: St. Martin's Press, 1982

Holtz, Herman. *The Complete Work-at-Home Companion.* Rocklin, Calif.: PrimaPub and Communications, 1990.

Partow, Donna. *Homemade Business.* Colorado Springs, Colo.: Focus on the Family, 1992.

Yater, Jan. *Making Your Office Work for You.* New York: Doubleday, 1989.

ELEVEN
Getting the Support You Need

Edwards, Paul and Sarah. *Working from Home: Everything You Need to Know about Living and Working under the Same Roof.* Los Angeles: J. P. Tarcher, 1990.